JESSICA SANDERS

Passive Income Ideas

Copyright © 2019 by Jessica Sanders

All rights reserved. No part of this publication may be reproduced, stored or transmitted in any form or by any means, electronic, mechanical, photocopying, recording, scanning, or otherwise without written permission from the publisher. It is illegal to copy this book, post it to a website, or distribute it by any other means without permission.

Jessica Sanders asserts the moral right to be identified as the author of this work.

Jessica Sanders has no responsibility for the persistence or accuracy of URLs for external or third-party Internet Websites referred to in this publication and does not guarantee that any content on such Websites is, or will remain, accurate or appropriate.

Designations used by companies to distinguish their products are often claimed as trademarks. All brand names and product names used in this book and on its cover are trade names, service marks, trademarks and registered trademarks of their respective owners. The publishers and the book are not associated with any product or vendor mentioned in this book. None of the companies referenced within the book have endorsed the book.

This document is geared towards providing exact and reliable information in regards to the topic and issue covered. The publication is sold with the idea that the publisher is not required to render accounting, officially permitted, or otherwise, qualified services. If advice is necessary, legal or professional, a practiced individual in the profession should be ordered.

From a Declaration of Principles which was accepted and approved equally by a Committee of the American Bar Association and a Committee of Publishers and Associations.

In no way is it legal to reproduce, duplicate, or transmit any part of this document in either electronic means or in printed format. Recording of this publication is strictly prohibited and any storage of this document is not allowed unless with written permission from the publisher. All rights reserved.

The information provided herein is stated to be truthful and consistent, in that any liability, in terms of inattention or otherwise, by any usage or abuse of any policies, processes, or directions contained within is the solitary and utter responsibility of the recipient reader. Under no circumstances will any legal responsibility or blame be held against the publisher for any reparation, damages, or monetary loss due to the information herein, either directly or indirectly.

Respective authors own all copyrights not held by the publisher.

The information herein is offered for informational purposes solely, and is universal as so. The presentation of the information is without contract or any type of guarantee assurance.

The trademarks that are used are without any consent, and the publication of the trademark is without permission or backing by the trademark owner. All trademarks and brands within this book are for clarifying purposes only and are the owned by the owners themselves, not affiliated with this document.

First edition

This book was professionally typeset on Reedsy.
Find out more at reedsy.com

Contents

PASSIVE INCOME OVERVIEW	1
DIVIDEND STOCKS	3
HIGH YIELD SAVINGS ACCOUNT AND MONEY MARKET FUNDS	9
CD LADDERS	13
ANNUITIES	16
INVEST IN REAL ESTATE INVESTMENT TRUST	40
REFINANCE YOUR MORTGAGE	45
PAY OFF OR REDUCE DEBT	50
INVEST IN A BUSINESS	54
SELL AN EBOOK ONLINE	58
CREATE A COURSE ON UDEMY	62
CREATE AN APP	65
AFFILIATE MARKETING	75
NETWORK MARKETING	92
DESIGN T-SHIRTS	99
SELL DIGITAL FILES ON ETSY	113
LIST PLACE ON AIRBNB	120

PASSIVE INCOME OVERVIEW

Passive income is highly sought after and often misunderstood.

Passive income streams require an upfront investment and an lot of nurturing in the beginning.

After some time and hard work, these income streams start to build and are able to maintain themselves, bringing you consistent revenue without much effort on your part.

Speaking from personal experience, adding passive income streams to your portfolio can help you increase your earnings and accelerate your financial goals in tremendous ways.

For example, you can use passive income streams to help you get out of debt or achieve financial independence sooner.

Like Fundrise - you can start investing in real estate for just $500. This is one of my favorite ways to build passive income.

Let me ask you a few questions.

Are you interested in earning money without having to kill yourself working for it?

Does the idea of having money coming in on a regular basis get you excited?

Are you tired of being paid based on how many hours of work you've put in?

If so, you should consider becoming involved with something that will earn you passive income.

Passive income is revenue that continues to come in over time after you have done a minimal amount of work.

Minimal means that the most work you will do will be at the beginning of your venture. Once you are set up, there is little maintenance work that will need to be done.

In most cases, weekly maintenance is enough to keep the money flowing. There are many passive income ideas to take into consideration.

This book will cover 16 passive income ideas.

DIVIDEND STOCKS

"When reward is at its pinnacle, risk is near at hand." - John Bogle, founder of Vanguard Group

Appreciating the fears many investors have, diversifying your portfolio is a good strategy to survive market instability.

There are plenty of choices for diversification- stocks, bonds, mutual and exchange- traded funds, Canadian income trusts, and many others.

For many investors, dividend stocks offer the best possible balance of risk and return.

Dividends are Attractive

Dividend stocks pay out distributions to shareholders.

Through dividend payments, a company distributes a portion of its earnings to its shareholders on a regular basis and re-invests the remaining profit into company's operating activities to fuel its continuing growth.

Consequently, investors benefit from both: share price appreciation and profit generation without selling shares.

Dividend stocks are a good investment choice in today's market climate.

They provide a steady flow of passive income, which you can either spend or reinvest (Personally I choose to reinvest my dividends back into my stocks).

Therefore, this type of stocks is particularly attractive to retirees aiming to earn some supplemental income.

Divide and Conquer!

Beware of over-concentration in your portfolio. Do not fill your investment basket with dividend stocks from only one company, sector, or industry.

By diversifying your portfolio you are not only increasing your wealth accumulation opportunities, but also lower your profile risk.

On one hand, companies that pay dividends are considered to be more stable than those that do not.

Startups usually do not make distributions among their shareholders, because they reinvest the entire profit in company's growth.

Once the company has attained a sustainable level of growth and success, the board of directors can vote to pay dividends to shareholders.

In this manner, the company maintains constant tight relationship with its shareholders.

On the other hand, companies are not legally required to pay dividends- they are optional.

In most cases dividends are paid only when the company has sufficient money to cover its operating cost.

If the management decides that the profit can be better utilized, dividend payments can be cut or held for a while.

Touchstones of Dividend Stocks

Looking for a promising dividend stock, the investor has to focus on the following three criteria: payout ratio, yield, and dividend growth.

Payout ratio is the percentage of a company's profit that is paid out as a dividend to shareholders.

A higher ratio is better. Payout percentage between 60% and 80% speaks highly for the company's financial health, but if it exceeds 100% it is a red flag.

More than 100% payout ratio means that the money is not coming from profit.

Most likely the company has financial difficulties and borrows money, which means is going into debt.

The second factor that has to be considered is the percentage return on your investment- yield.

High- yield dividend stock is a sign of a well- managed company that demonstrates consistent growth and the possibility dividend payments to be increased are relatively high.

This brings us to the third criteria- dividend growth, which measures a company's ability to earn ever- increasing profits and shares ever- increasing dividends with shareholders.

Dividend Investing for Your Portfolio

All in all, dividend investing can be a great way to mitigate risk, as well as provide a steady stream of income from your investments.

Investors simply need to remember the three basic touchstones above and invest wisely.

Reasons to Own Dividend Stocks

One mistake many beginner investor makes is ignoring dividends.

Sure, it may seem dividends are only a small part of any stock portfolio - everyone wants to see the price go up, up and up!

But smart investors (or those who want to be) listen up: When it comes to long-term investing, dividend stocks have their advantage - after all, when was the last time someone PAID you for owning something?

When doing some stock market investing, it's best to look to the future, and what dividend stocks can do for you. Here are three reasons why you should buy into dividend stocks:

1. (Almost) Risk-Free Stock Market Investing

There's no such thing as 100% safe when you invest, but when a company has enough funds to pay out their investors, then it is most likely a strong company.

Most dividend stocks are companies with solid backgrounds, and can withstand most economic situations. Because they are making good profits, and are able to pay their expenses and STILL have excess income to share with their investors, then you know this a great company.

Between a company who pays out dividends and one with a stock price that fluctuates - which one do you think has a better chance of protecting your capital?

2. Increase Capital Gains

Some companies offer DRIPs or dividend reinvestment plans.

Basically, instead of paying you the cash out, your share of the dividends gets reinvested to buy you MORE stock - that means you are essentially getting stock FOR FREE.

And when that stock price goes up, then more capital gains for you. Eventually, this type of plan can benefit you when doing long-term investing.

3. Dividend stocks = passive income

Can you imagine, sitting on the beach, sipping a margarita and money keeps going into your bank account.

Dividends are income which are handed to you on a silver platter - without you having to lift a finger!

Aside from what you're reaping from increasing stock prices, you get a regular payment in form of dividends. Buy more of the dividend stock and you get even more income.

Do whatever you want with it - use it to pay debt, buy a fancy car or, if you were thinking of long-term investing, set up a system where you take your payments and invest in more dividend stocks.

When you have enough shares, well then just keep sipping that margarita on the beach and enjoy your income!

Of course, when the economy is not doing so well, a company can cut back on its dividends.

Still, a successful value investing strategy require smart investors to know that dividend stocks which have a high yield is a way to collect income from a source which will be around for a long time.

If you are new to stocks and dividends, I highly recommend joining the Top Dividends community.

They provide you with the Top 100 Dividend Stocks for a small monthly fee. Also you will be provided with monthly paying dividend stocks, safe dividend stock ratings and more.

Join Here: ———> http://bit.ly/topdividendsstocks

HIGH YIELD SAVINGS ACCOUNT AND MONEY MARKET FUNDS

With near-zero interest rates have been the norm for some time, you have probably been conditioned to accept rates on your liquid cash that barely register on your account statements.

According to bankrate.com, the average money market account (MMA) rate in the nation was 0.20%, when checked on August 29, 2018, which would earn $20 on a $10,000 deposit after the first year.

You can find better rates by shopping and comparing. If you're willing to do your banking in the Internet cloud, you can sometimes find MMA rates topping 2.0%.

However, there's another option that can have even better rates: high-interest checking accounts.

These can pay in the 3% to 5% range and are usually found at smaller community banks, credit unions or online banks.

It is easy to become captivated by the comparatively alluring rates they offer, but, with all the caveats involved, they are definitely not for everyone.

Money Market Account

Money market accounts are federally insured short-term interest-bearing instruments that generate a variable yield while preserving principal.

They tend to deliver interest rates that are higher than those for savings accounts, but they also often call for a higher minimum deposit.

Some require a minimum balance to receive the highest rate. The interest rates on MMAs are variable, which means they rise and fall with the interest rate market.

Most MMAs come with limited check writing and balance transfer privileges. However, federal regulations limit the number of transactions in MMAs to six a month.

High-Interest Checking Account

High-interest checking accounts have all the trappings that normally come with regular checking accounts.

Many offer unlimited checks, a debit card, online account management and perks such as rewards points and free overdraft protection.

Many will waive the monthly maintenance fee if you maintain a minimum daily balance.

The accounts are usually capped, meaning that the higher interest rate is paid only up to a certain level of money on deposit.

Most accounts are capped at $25,000, but the caps can go as low as $1,000. Deposits that exceed the cap earn a much lower rate, as low as

0.1%.

Which Is Better?

Although high-interest checking accounts offer rates that are significantly higher than those available on savings accounts or MMAs, you have to meet a number of conditions to earn a higher rate.

For instance, with many high-interest checking accounts, you must accept direct deposit and electronic statements.

Many accounts require 10 transactions; if you only make nine, you lose the higher rate for the statement period.

And these accounts sometimes require at least one bill pay or transfer from the account per statement period.

Though none of these requirements are insurmountable, meeting them means that you have to actively manage the account.

Most people are used to a more passive approach to account management.

An MMA is generally a better option if you want to park some cash for a short period, or if you don't want to actively manage your savings.

It gives you access to your money when you need it while requiring a minimum amount of effort on your part.

If you're willing to manage your account actively, a high-interest checking account can generate significantly higher interest earnings than a typical MMA.

If in the normal course of a month, you expect to make the required number of debit transactions and have at least one bill you can set up on automatic bill payment, a high-interest checking account shouldn't be much to manage.

The most difficult aspect is the cap. To optimize your interest rate earnings, you need to make sure that the amount on deposit doesn't exceed the cap.

You will likely need to keep transferring from lower-yielding accounts to ensure you maximize the amount that can be earning the higher yield.

For a $10,000 deposit in a high-interest checking account earning 2.5% interest, that is about $240 more in earnings than a typical MMA.

The Bottom Line

High-interest checking accounts and money market accounts can both earn you more in interest than a plain old savings account.

The former takes more effort on your part but can result in the highest yields. The latter has the advantage of not needing constant oversight.

They still give you access to your money when you need it, like a savings account, but earn a better, though variable, rate of interest.

Each is a good reason not to leave all of your hard-earned money sitting in a savings account, where it can barely earn interest at all.

CD LADDERS

A CD ladder is a strategy in which an investor divides the amount of money to be invested into equal amounts in certificates of deposit (CDs) with different maturity dates.

This strategy decreases both interest rate and re-investment risks.

BREAKING DOWN CD Ladder

A Certificate of Deposit (CD) is an investment product that offers a fixed interest rate for a specified period of time.

The invested funds, which are insured up to $250,000 by the Federal Deposit Insurance Corporation (FDIC), are locked in by the issuing bank until the maturity date of the CD.

Maturity dates for these savings instruments are typically set at three months, six months, one year, or five years.

The higher the term for which funds are committed, the higher the interest paid.

To take advantage of the various interest rates offered for different periods, investors can follow a strategy known as the CD ladder.

A CD ladder strategy is followed by investors who value the safety of their principal and income.

This strategy also provides investors with steady cash flow as the CDs will mature at different times.

An investor that incorporates this strategy will allocate the same amount of funds across CDs with different maturities.

This way, s/he benefits from the higher interest rates of longer-term CDs and does not have to repeatedly renew a short-term certificate of deposit that holds all his or her funds.

Investors that put all their funds in one CD may miss out on higher interest rates that may result while their funds are locked away.

With a CD ladder, however, the investor can take advantage of short-term interest rates by reinvesting proceeds from maturing CDs into newer CDs with higher interest rates.

On the other hand, if interest rates fall, CD holders still enjoy the benefits of the high interest rates that their existing long-term CDs provide.

A CD ladder, thus, provides regular opportunities to reinvest cash as the CDs mature, while reducing interest rate risk.

In the event that an emergency ensues and an investor needs cash, the laddering strategy ensures that the investor consistently has a CD maturing, thereby, reducing liquidity risk.

For example, an investor has $40,000 to invest.

Rather than putting the entire funds in one CD, he decides to put

CD LADDERS

$10,000 in each of four certificates of deposit maturing in 6 months, 12 months, 18 months, and 24 months.

ANNUITIES

An annuity is simply a way of providing a regular income. This is most typically to provide an individual with income once they have stopped working.

There are two basic types of annuity: Pension Annuities and Purchased Life Annuities

Pension annuities

Pension Annuities can only be bought with money/funds held within registered pension plans/ schemes.

In practice pension annuities fall into two types - lifetime annuities and scheme pensions. They are similar in that they provide an income for life but they have different rules. The differences are even more marked following the Taxation of Pensions Act 2014.

Although historically we use the term "pension annuity" where the rules apply equally to the scheme pension and the lifetime annuity, great care should be taken as scheme pensions do not enjoy much of the flexibility now available for lifetime annuities.

Scheme Pensions

A Scheme Pension is a pension income payable either from the scheme itself or from an insurance company selected by the scheme.

Defined Benefit schemes can only provide pension income via a scheme pension.

If the member wishes to access the flexibilities now offered under lifetime annuities they must transfer their benefits prior to crystallisation.

It is possible for a money purchase/defined contribution pension scheme to provide a scheme pension, but a scheme pension may only be paid if the member had an opportunity to select a lifetime annuity instead.

Scheme pensions must:

• Be paid at least annually, and

• Not have a guaranteed period of more than 10 years

• Not reduce unless in specified circumstances (changes to income), and

• Be paid by the scheme administrator or an insurance company selected by them.

• The rules governing scheme pensions are generally more restrictive than those for lifetime annuities.

Lifetime Annuities

Lifetime Annuities are payable by an insurance company where the member had the right to choose the insurance company.

The member's right to choose the insurance company is a key difference compared to scheme pensions.

Prior to 6 April 2015 the basic rules applying to a lifetime annuity require that:

• It was paid by an insurance company

• The member could choose the insurance company

• It was payable at least annually and for life

• If it had a minimum guaranteed period, that period was not more than 10 years

• The amount of annuity either could not decrease or could change only in accordance with specific rules set out in regulations

• The potential survivor of a joint life annuity was usually limited to a formal dependant of the member

• It couldn't create a lump sum on death (other than capital protection)

• It couldn't be surrendered or assigned, although this was possible through the will for guaranteed periods or to comply with a pensions sharing order.

This is also the current situation, but please see the post-6 April 2015 rules for important proposals.

• If it has a minimum guaranteed period, that period needn't be limited to 10 years annuities now have a wider definition of allowed decreases the potential survivor of a joint life annuity needn't be a formal dependant of the member.

Previous limitations on the term 'dependant', (spouse, civil partner, child under age 23 etc.) no longer apply to lifetime annuities. The annuitant can select anyone to become a joint annuitant.

However, this will be subject to acceptance by the provider and may have an impact of the amount of annuity payable.

In addition to the survivor's joint life annuity, which can be paid to a dependant or nominee, if there are any unused pension funds available on the death of a member (they could be uncrystallised funds or unused drawdown funds that haven't been used in the provision of a dependant or nominee annuity) they can be used to provide a successor's annuity.

A lifetime annuity can't create a lump sum on death. A lifetime annuity can't be surrendered or assigned, although this is possible through the will for guaranteed periods or to comply with a pensions sharing order.

See Finance Act 2004: Sch 28, Para 3 (as amended by the Taxation of Pensions Act 2014)

A section 32 buyout policy will provide a lifetime annuity because the member will be able to transfer it to another insurance company to pay the income – i.e. the member can choose the insurance company that ultimately pays the annuity.

How the law allows annuity income to vary

Scheme Pensions

The law is fairly restrictive on when it allows an amount of scheme pension to change. There is no room for variation (unlike with Lifetime

Annuities) and the legislation states the circumstances where Scheme Pensions may be reduced or stopped.

There are currently 9 situations where a Scheme Pension may be reduced or stopped:

• The reduction of the pension if the member became entitled to it by reason of the ill-health condition being met

• All the members in the scheme are having their pensions reduced at the same time

• It was a bridging pension and state pension age has been reached

• On wind up where the scheme cannot support paying the pensions at their existing level

• Subsequent to a pension sharing order being applied to the pension

• A court order has directed so

• On abatement. This applies to public sector schemes where the member returns to employment in the public sector and means their pension may be reduced

• Reduction due to forfeiting benefits

• The reduction of the pension in any other circumstances prescribed by regulations made by the Board of Inland Revenue See Finance Act 2004: Sch 28, Para 2(4) (as amended by the Taxation of Pensions Act 2014)

Finance Act 2005: Para 11(6) and (7)

The Pension Schemes (Reduction in Pension rates) Regulations 2006 - SI 2006/138 as amended by SI 2009/1311

Lifetime Annuities

A lifetime annuity may increase or decrease in line with any one or a combination of the following:

• Retail prices index/consumer prices index

• The value of 'freely marketable assets' (e.g. shares, OEICs, Unit Trusts, unit-linked pension funds)

• An index of 'freely marketable assets' (e.g. FTSE 100, Dow Jones Industrial Average)

With-Profits funds

After allowance for any contractual charges

Conventional lifetime annuities purchased prior to April 2015 are annuities which do not decrease, or any falls are determined by regulations made by the Board of Inland Revenue.

However, The Taxation of Pension Act 2014 details changes to annuities that are purchased post April 2015.

From 6th April 2015, in addition to reductions determined by the Board of Inland Revenue, annuities can decrease by "allowed decreases", which widens the circumstances in which annuities can reduce.

Exactly what annuity options will be made available by providers under the relaxed legislation is yet to be clarified.

Notwithstanding the annuity design possibilities of the change in the post April 2015 legislation, detailed above, different annuity contracts may currently use different methods. The following methodology will continue for annuities purchased pre April 2015.

They can:

• Move fully in line with the change in the linked investments/index

• Vary based on the anticipated growth of the linked investment / index

• Have maximum and minimum income limits that are reviewed at regular intervals based on the value of the underlying investment / index (See Finance Act 2004: Sch 28, Para 3(1)(d) (as amended by the Taxation of Pensions Act 2014) Finance Act 2005: Sch 10, Para 13(2) and (4)

The Registered Pension Schemes (Prescribed Manner of Determining Amount of Annuities) Regulations 2006 - SI 2006/568

1. Fully Linked

Fully linked annuities operate just as it says. The annuity income will rise and fall based on the increase or decrease in the underlying investment or index. An example is an inflation-linked annuity.

Inflation-Linked Annuities

As the name suggests, inflation-linked annuities vary according to the rate of inflation.

This is usually the retail prices index (RPI) but could also be the consumer prices index (CPI).

This provides protection against the effects of inflation – an annuity linked to RPI will increase by 3.8% in a year if RPI is 3.8% for that year.

The change will usually apply at each one year anniversary of the date the annuity started.

The starting level of an inflation-linked annuity will depend to some extent on the provider's view of future inflation.

It may start higher or lower than a fixed escalating annuity depending on the rate of fixed escalation chosen.

For example, an annuity increasing by 5% pa might have a lower starting level than an inflation-linked annuity, but one with a 2% pa fixed escalation may have a higher starting level.

POINT TO NOTE: the relative difference in the starting level of a fixed escalating annuity and an inflation-linked annuity will vary depending on economic outlook/circumstances and may change over time - it is important not to assume one will always start higher than the other.

In a period of deflation (i.e. negative inflation) an inflation-linked annuity may be expected to reduce.

For example, if inflation is -2.4% in a year, the annuity would reduce by 2.4%. However, some inflation-linked annuities are written so that they will not reduce even where there is deflation - the annuity will remain at its previous level instead.

POINT TO NOTE: pensioner inflation (inflation for those who are older) tends to be higher than the general measure of RPI or CPI. This means that while an inflation-linked annuity may keep pace with inflation generally that does not mean it will keep pace with inflation for the individual.

2. Investment-Linked Annuities

Investment-linked annuities are those that can alter in accordance with: the value of 'freely marketable assets' (e.g. shares, OEICs, Unit Trusts, unit-linked pension funds); or an index of 'freely marketable assets' (e.g. FTSE 100, Dow Jones Industrial Average)

With-Profits funds

After allowance for any contractual charges

The most common are unit-linked annuities and with-profits annuities.

While investment-linked annuities can, and do, use different underlying investments to determine the amount of annuity payable, they all operate using the same general principles:

• A starting level of income is chosen, usually by the individual from a range set by the annuity provider

• The starting level will equate to a certain rate of growth each year – sometimes referred to as the anticipated growth rate

• The actual rate of growth each year is determined by the growth on the underlying investments chosen - e.g. with-profits fund, unit linked funds

- If the actual rate of growth each year is the same as the anticipated growth rate the annuity will remain level

- If the actual rate of growth each year is lower than the anticipated growth rate the annuity will reduce

- If the actual rate of growth each year is higher than the anticipated growth rate the annuity will increase

POINT TO NOTE: the starting level of an investment-linked annuity will vary depending on the anticipated growth rate (AGR) chosen at the start.

For a fund of £100,000 the starting annuity will be higher if an AGR of 6% is chosen as compared to an AGR of 2%.

As a general rule, as the chosen AGR gets higher the starting annuity will become closer to the annuity provided through a fixed level annuity.

It is usually possible to select an AGR that will provide a starting annuity of the same amount as a fixed level annuity.

Investment-linked annuities do carry investment risk which neither fixed nor inflation-linked annuities have.

This investment risk may help combat the effects of inflation, whilst also providing the opportunity for the individual's money to still be linked with investment performance. The client's income will vary in accordance with investment performance.

POINT TO NOTE: The difference in starting annuity, based on the anticipated growth rate (AGR) chosen, reflects the level of investment risk being taken.

The higher the AGR, the higher the investment risk, the greater the chance of the annuity reducing in future, the lower the chance of it increasing in future.

A balance has therefore to be struck between the level of risk a client is willing / able to accept, the AGR and the starting level of the annuity.

3. Variable Annuities

Variable annuities offer an alternative 'middle ground' between conventional (fixed/inflation-linked) annuities and income drawdown.

In a similar manner to investment-linked annuities they offer the ability for a continued link between the annuity income and investment performance.

However, they go one step further than investment-linked annuities in that they can provide wider income limits, have greater income variability and allow for income reviews to be undertaken, all of which are similar in nature to the old rules that were applicable to income drawdown.

Variable annuities are not, however, able to replicate all of the death benefits permitted under income drawdown; in particular, they are not able to return a lump sum on death as income drawdown can.

The income from a variable annuity can be chosen from within a set range which is 50% - 120% of the amount of level annuity the fund could purchase with the variable annuity provider

If the variable annuity provider does not offer level annuities itself the limits will be calculated based on the average of three current market annuity rates for a level annuity.

The individual may choose an income at any point between these limits and can vary the amount of income at any time agreed with the annuity provider, as long as it stays within the above limits.

The minimum and maximum income range/limits must themselves be reviewed by the annuity provider at least once every 3 years.

That review will set the minimum and maximum for the period until the next review date.

POINT TO NOTE: At the outset the fund used to calculate the income limits will be an actual pension fund but at future reviews it will be a notional fund.

This is because an annuity contract does not have an actual fund value as such - if it did then it would not qualify as an annuity under tax law.

The money has been used at the outset to buy the lifetime annuity but a notional fund value will be maintained and used when calculating the income limits at subsequent reviews.

When the amount of annuity has been chosen the same basic approach to investment returns, as that for investment-linked annuities, can be applied.

The notional fund is linked to underlying investments, such as a with-profits fund or unit-linked funds, and the value of that notional fund will go up or down in line with their investment performance.

The annuity is paid from that notional fund and so will also impact its value.

If the value increases, the income limits at a review will also increase, thus increasing the maximum annuity that may be paid.

If the value reduces, the income limits at the next review will also decrease, thus decreasing the maximum annuity that may be paid

It is therefore possible for the notional fund under a variable annuity to increase or reduce significantly depending on the level of annuity and investment performance.

POINT TO NOTE: this means that the level of investment risk associated with a variable annuity is higher compared to an investment-linked annuity with an investment-linked annuity the amount of annuity previously paid out does not have any effect on the possible future annuity, but under a variable annuity it does.

POINT TO NOTE: variable annuities provide a solution to the lack of flexibility in being able to alter income, which is associated with other annuities.

They provide a further step toward income drawdown although their inability to offer the same range of death benefits as income drawdown mean they will not be appropriate for those to whom the death benefit is the key factor.

4. Other Annuity Types

Conventional Annuities

As detailed above, prior to 6 April 2015, conventional annuities could not usually decrease. This limitation will continue to apply to conventional annuities purchased prior to 6th April 2015.

Although post 6 April 2015 annuities are allowed to reduce by "allowed decreases", at the time of writing (April 2015), it is still unclear what impact this will have on the shape of annuity products offered by providers.

In respect to conventional annuities issued prior to 6 April 2015, they fall into one of two basic varieties: Those that remain level throughout the time they are paid; or those that increase by a fixed amount/rate at set intervals.

A level annuity will pay the same amount throughout the period it is paid.

A fixed increasing (also known as an escalating) annuity will normally increase by a set percentage each year, on a compound basis.

POINT TO NOTE: a level annuity will generally provide the highest starting amount of annuity as compared to most other annuities (variable annuities being a notable exception).

This is because if increasing annuity options are incorporated, the cost of providing those must be met and that is through the starting level of annuity.

So, an increasing annuity will have a lower, possibly much lower, starting point than a level annuity.

The risk of the amount of a conventional annuity reducing is very low - that would only potentially happen if the provider paying the annuity became insolvent.

Even in that scenario the protection afforded by the Financial Services Compensation Scheme is 90% of the annuity value.

POINT TO NOTE: This credit risk applies to all annuities, not just fixed annuities.

Guaranteed Pension Annuities do, however, carry an inflation risk. Inflation erodes the purchasing power of money over time - £100 in today's money will buy you less than £100 in, say, 5 years' time because of the effects of inflation on the cost of living.

So an annuity that is level will lose its value over time, where inflation is positive.

An increasing annuity provides some protection against this, although the level of that protection depends on the difference between the rate of fixed increases and the rate of inflation -- if the rate of inflation is higher than the rate of escalation, the annuity will reduce in value over time and vice versa.

Protected Rights Annuities

Annuities paid from 'protected rights' pension funds are subject to some specific legislation.

If the member is married the annuity must include a survivor's annuity where a guaranteed period is included it cannot be more than 5 years.

The Personal and Occupational Pension Schemes (Protected Rights) Regulations 1996, SI 1996/1537

Historically there were greater restrictions on protected rights annuities, but these have been removed gradually over time.

There are no longer any other legal restrictions regarding the form of protected rights annuities and so all of the other options described above are available.

Protected Rights were abolished from April 2012, at which time the above restrictions also disappeared.

However, protected rights annuities already set up will continue to operate on the basis they were set up.

Enhanced and Impaired Life Annuities

Enhanced Annuities are annuities that provide higher amounts than a 'normal' annuity because of the individual having a lower than 'normal' life expectancy.

This reduced life expectancy could be due to long-standing lifestyle or health issues. For example, smokers, those with high blood pressure or relating to the specific health of the individual.

Enhanced annuities usually operate on the basis of a standard, higher, annuity rate being applied.

For example, a smoker may get a set annuity rate, which is higher than for a non-smoker.

There is no assessment of the individual's health as the enhanced rate is a 'standard' enhancement to the ordinary annuity rate.

Impaired life annuities are, however, specific to the individual.

They involve an underwriting assessment of the individual in order to assess his or her life expectancy, based on his or her own health.

A higher annuity rate might then be offered as a result of that assessment.

POINT TO NOTE: the terms 'enhanced' and 'impaired life' have tended to become mixed over time.

The introduction of 'post code pricing' has not helped as these could potentially be regarded as 'enhanced' annuities.

The terms are, perhaps, irrelevant, though as the most important point is if the individual will get a higher annuity because of his/her health.

Factors influencing the annuity amount

There are 3 main factors affecting the amount of annuity income payable from the annuity purchase price:

1. Life expectancy

This is linked to age, health and, until 1st December 2012, gender.

Age

Annuities are a guarantee of an income for life, therefore the rates they're based on change as life expectancy increases.

The younger people are when they retire, the longer they are likely to have in retirement and the longer the annuity is likely to be payable.

For this reason, a 60 year old will generally receive a lower income than a 70 year old.

Health

If the prospective annuitant, or one or both joint life annuitants or the dependant of an annuitant has a medical or lifestyle condition they may qualify for an increased income through 'enhanced' terms. This normally pays a higher income.

Gender

Until 21 December 2012 annuity rates could be based on gender. Generally, females received less income as they lived for longer.

Since then annuity rates must be on a gender neutral basis by law.

2. Gilt Yields

Gilts are government bonds. The government issues gilts to raise money – in return they pay an amount of interest.

In conventional Gilts this amount is fixed for the lifetime of the bond and is known as the coupon. For example, the government may issue Treasury 5% 2026.

This shows who issued the Gilt (Treasury), the interest rate to be paid (relative to the initial price) and when it is due to be repaid.

This means it has a coupon rate of 5% based on the initial nominal value of £100. £5 per annum will be paid out to the holder of the gilt until 2026 when the government will repay the £100 – a 5% yield.

After being issued by the Debt Management Office in the first instance, Gilts can then be traded on the secondary market where the demand for and supply of them will determine their value.

If demand increases then prices rise so yields fall and vice versa. This means a good day for bond holders will see the asking price of their bonds go up but their running yield fall.

Therefore a fall in bond yields is not necessarily bad news and may be good news depending on your objective.

As well as those conventional Gilts discussed above there are index-linked gilts, double-dated gilts and undated gilts.

Of these the index-linked is most common making up around 30% of the Gilt market. There are very few double-dated and undated Gilts remaining.

Annuity providers predominately buy gilts to match their annuity liabilities. Therefore, movement in yields will impact the annuity rates offered. Lower yields = lower rates and vice versa

3. Options chosen

There are many options available with annuities. They can be:

• Single life or joint life (post 6th April the joint annuitant, subject to the provider's approval, may be anyone selected by the annuitant.

The selected age etc. of the joint annuitant may have a significant impact on the initial annuity, for example if the annuitant selects a grandchild as a joint annuitant, the initial annuity will be considerably lower than if the joint annuitant was of a similar age to the member).

• Guaranteed or not guaranteed (previous 10 year limit no longer applies to new annuities purchased post 6th April 2015)

• Escalating or not escalating

- Frequency of payments

- Whether payment is in advance or in arrears

- With or without overlap

The more options added the lower the income will be. Likewise, the type of option taken has an impact.

For example, a 15 year guaranteed annuity will pay less initial annuity than a 5 year guaranteed annuity and a joint life annuity where there is no reduction on death would pay less than one with a 50% reduction on death. (Please note that for annuities arranged after 6th April 2015 there is no limit on the guaranteed period that can be built into a Lifetime Annuity, subject to being offered by provider).

- Invest Automatically in the stock market

The lure of big money has always thrown investors into the lap of stock markets. However, making money in equities is not easy.

It not only requires oodles of patience and discipline, but also a great deal of research and a sound understanding of the market, among others.

Added to this is the fact that stock market volatility in the last few years has left investors in a state of confusion.

They are in a dilemma whether to invest, hold or sell in such a scenario.

1. Avoid the herd mentality

The typical buyer's decision is usually heavily influenced by the actions of his acquaintances, neighbours or relatives.

Thus, if everybody around is investing in a particular stock, the tendency for potential investors is to do the same. But this strategy is bound to backfire in the long run.

No need to say that you should always avoid having the herd mentality if you don't want to lose your hard-earned money in stock markets.

The world's greatest investor Warren Buffett was surely not wrong when he said, "Be fearful when others are greedy, and be greedy when others are fearful!"

2. Take informed decision

Proper research should always be undertaken before investing in stocks. But that is rarely done.

Investors generally go by the name of a company or the industry they belong to. This is, however, not the right way of putting one's money into the stock market.

3. Invest in business you understand

Never invest in a stock. Invest in a business instead. And invest in a business you understand. In other words, before investing in a company, you should know what business the company is in.

4. Don't try to time the market

One thing that even Warren Buffett doesn't do is to try to time the stock market, although he does have a very strong view on the price levels appropriate to individual shares.

A majority of investors, however, do just the opposite, something that financial planners have always been warning them to avoid, and thus lose their hard-earned money in the process.

"So, you should never try to time the market. In fact, nobody has ever done this successfully and consistently over multiple business or stock market cycles. Catching the tops and bottoms is a myth.

It is so till today and will remain so in the future. In fact, in doing so, more people have lost far more money than people who have made money," says Anil Chopra, group CEO and director, Bajaj Capital.

5. Follow a disciplined investment approach

Historically it has been witnessed that even great bull runs have shown bouts of panic moments.

The volatility witnessed in the markets has inevitably made investors lose money despite the great bull runs.

However, the investors who put in money systematically, in the right shares and held on to their investments patiently have been seen generating outstanding returns.

Hence, it is prudent to have patience and follow a disciplined investment approach besides keeping a long-term broad picture in mind.

6. Do not let emotions cloud your judgement

Many investors have been losing money in stock markets due to their inability to control emotions, particularly fear and greed. In a bull market, the lure of quick wealth is difficult to resist.

Greed augments when investors hear stories of fabulous returns being made in the stock market in a short period of time. "This leads them to speculate, buy shares of unknown companies or create heavy positions in the futures segment without really understanding the risks involved," says Kapur.

Instead of creating wealth, these investors thus burn their fingers very badly the moment the sentiment in the market reverses.

In a bear market, on the other hand, investors panic and sell their shares at rock-bottom prices. Thus, fear and greed are the worst emotions to feel when investing, and it is better not to be guided by them.

7. Create a broad portfolio

Diversification of portfolio across asset classes and instruments is the key factor to earn optimum returns on investments with minimum risk. Level of diversification depends on each investor's risk taking capacity.

8. Have realistic expectations

There's nothing wrong with hoping for the 'best' from your investments, but you could be heading for trouble if your financial goals are based on unrealistic assumptions.

For instance, lots of stocks have generated more than 50 per cent returns during the great bull run of recent years.

However, it doesn't mean that you should always expect the same kind of return from the stock markets.

Therefore, when Warren Buffett says that earning more than 12 per cent in stock is pure dumb luck and you laugh at it, you're surely inviting trouble for yourself.

9. Invest only your surplus funds

If you want to take risk in a volatile market like this, then see whether you have surplus funds which you can afford to lose. It is not necessary that you will lose money in the present scenario.

You investments can give you huge gains too in the months to come.

But no one can be hundred percent sure. That is why you will have to take risk. No need to say that invest only if you are flush with surplus funds.

10. Monitor rigorously

We are living in a global village. Any important event happening in any part of the world has an impact on our financial markets.

Hence we need to constantly monitor our portfolio and keep affecting the desired changes in it.

If you can't review your portfolio due to time constraint or lack of knowledge, then you should take the help of a good financial planner or someone who is capable of doing that. "If you can't even do that, then stock investing is not for you.

Better put your money in safe or less-risky instruments," advises Kapur.

INVEST IN REAL ESTATE INVESTMENT TRUST

Real estate investment trusts ("REITs") allow individuals to invest in large-scale, income-producing real estate.

A REIT is a company that owns and typically operates income-producing real estate or related assets. These may include office buildings, shopping malls, apartments, hotels, resorts, self-storage facilities, warehouses, and mortgages or loans. Unlike other real estate companies, a REIT does not develop real estate properties to resell them.

Instead, a REIT buys and develops properties primarily to operate them as part of its own investment portfolio.

Why Would Somebody Invest In REITs?

REITs provide a way for individual investors to earn a share of the income produced through commercial real estate ownership – without actually having to go out and buy commercial real estate.

What Types Of REITs Are There?

Many REITs are registered with the SEC and are publicly traded on a stock exchange. These are known as publicly traded REITs.

Others may be registered with the SEC but are not publicly traded. These are known as non-traded REITs (also known as non-exchange traded REITs).

This is one of the most important distinctions among the various kinds of REITs. Before investing in a REIT, you should understand whether or not it is publicly traded, and how this could affect the benefits and risks to you.

What Are The Benefits And Risks Of REITs?

REITs offer a way to include real estate in one's investment portfolio. Additionally, some REITs may offer higher dividend yields than some other investments.

But there are some risks, especially with non-exchange traded REITs. Because they do not trade on a stock exchange, non-traded REITs involve special risks:

Lack of Liquidity: Non-traded REITs are illiquid investments. They generally cannot be sold readily on the open market.

If you need to sell an asset to raise money quickly, you may not be able to do so with shares of a non-traded REIT.

Share Value Transparency: While the market price of a publicly traded REIT is readily accessible, it can be difficult to determine the value of a share of a non-traded REIT.

Non-traded REITs typically do not provide an estimate of their value per share until 18 months after their offering closes.

This may be years after you have made your investment. As a result, for a significant time period you may be unable to assess the value of your non-traded REIT investment and its volatility.

Distributions May Be Paid from Offering Proceeds and Borrowings: Investors may be attracted to non-traded REITs by their relatively high dividend yields compared to those of publicly traded REITs. Unlike publicly traded REITs, however, non-traded REITs frequently pay distributions in excess of their funds from operations.

To do so, they may use offering proceeds and borrowings.

This practice, which is typically not used by publicly traded REITs, reduces the value of the shares and the cash available to the company to purchase additional assets.

Conflicts of Interest: Non-traded REITs typically have an external manager instead of their own employees.

This can lead to potential conflicts of interests with shareholders.

For example, the REIT may pay the external manager significant fees based on the amount of property acquisitions and assets under management.

These fee incentives may not necessarily align with the interests of shareholders.

How To Buy And Sell REITs

You can invest in a publicly traded REIT, which is listed on a major stock exchange, by purchasing shares through a broker.

You can purchase shares of a non-traded REIT through a broker that participates in the non-traded REIT's offering.

You can also purchase shares in a REIT mutual fund or REIT exchange-traded fund.

Understanding Fees And Taxes

Publicly traded REITs can be purchased through a broker. Generally, you can purchase the common stock, preferred stock, or debt security of a publicly traded REIT.

Brokerage fees will apply.

Non-traded REITs are typically sold by a broker or financial adviser. Non-traded REITs generally have high up-front fees.

Sales commissions and upfront offering fees usually total approximately 9 to 10 percent of the investment. These costs lower the value of the investment by a significant amount.

Special Tax Considerations

Most REITS pay out at least 100 percent of their taxable income to their shareholders. The shareholders of a REIT are responsible for paying taxes on the dividends and any capital gains they receive in connection with their investment in the REIT.

Dividends paid by REITs generally are treated as ordinary income and are not entitled to the reduced tax rates on other types of corporate dividends.

Consider consulting your tax adviser before investing in REITs.

Avoiding Fraud

Be wary of any person who attempts to sell REITs that are not registered with the SEC.

You can verify the registration of both publicly traded and non-traded REITs through the SEC's EDGAR system.

You can also use EDGAR to review a REIT's annual and quarterly reports as well as any offering prospectus. For more on how to use EDGAR, please visit Research Public Companies.

You should also check out the broker or investment adviser who recommends purchasing a REIT.

REFINANCE YOUR MORTGAGE

You made it through one of the toughest challenges: buying a home. Now, perhaps just a few years later, you're ready to refinance your mortgage.

How hard can it be? You may be surprised to find that it's not a couple-of-emails-and-a-phone-call-or-two process.

In fact, there may be more paperwork involved this time around than when you first bought your home.

Let's consider some important initial steps of a mortgage refinance — and then run through the rest of the process step by step.

Why you might want to refinance

Before you begin, it's important to consider why you want to refinance your home loan in the first place. That guides the mortgage refinance process from the very beginning.

Lowering your payment is usually the goal. And it's tempting to refinance with another full 30-year term to really knock down that monthly payment.

But that means you'll end up taking even longer to pay off your house and paying more interest.

Choosing a suitable loan term for your mortgage refinance is a balancing act between an affordable monthly payment and reducing your borrowing costs.

You'll want to take into account how much interest you've already paid on your old loan and how much you'll pay with the refinance.

Loans are front-loaded with interest, so the longer you've been paying, the more each payment is going toward paying off the principal balance — and the more interest you've already paid.

Comparing what you've paid in interest so far and what you will pay on your current loan versus the refi will give you a solid idea of your total loan costs for either option.

By resisting the urge to extend your loan term, you can instead refinance to reduce the term and to get a lower interest rate, which could significantly reduce the amount of interest you pay over the life of the loan.

Choosing a suitable loan term for your mortgage refinance is a balancing act between an affordable monthly payment and reducing your borrowing costs.

Use a mortgage refinance calculator

Once you know you have a good reason and you've determined it's the right time to refinance, it's time to work the numbers. Using a mortgage refinance calculator can help you shop for the best mortgage.

You'll need to know (or make some educated guesses about) your new interest rate and your new loan amount.

After you input the data, the tool will calculate your monthly savings, new payment, and lifetime savings, taking into account the estimated costs of your refinance.

Working with a refinance calculator will give you a good idea of what to expect. Even better, when you have a few estimates from mortgage lenders you can enter the terms they offer you into the calculator to help determine which one offers the best deal.

It's also key to shop the best refinance rates

Now it's time for a little legwork — or more likely web work and phone calls. You want to shop for your best mortgage refinance rate and get a loan estimate from each lender.

Each potential lender is required to issue the estimate within three days of receiving your basic information.

The estimate is a pretty simple three-page document that details the loan terms, projected payments, estimated closing costs and other fees.

Compare the loan details from each lender and decide which one is best for you. This is a good time to really work that mortgage refinance calculator.

Refinancing your home loan, step by step

Ready to tackle the whole refinance process? Go!

Determine your goal. We've covered this: Refinance for the right reason. Aim to shorten — or at least maintain — your current loan term while lowering your interest rate.

Learn your current credit score. Check your credit history and get your credit score. The better your score, the better the mortgage refinance interest rates you'll be offered.

Research your home's current value. Check your neighborhood for recent sales of homes like yours. Estimate your home value with NerdWallet's free home value tool.

Shop for your best mortgage rate. Start by comparing refinance rates online.

You can shop rates online all you want, but limit the window for submitting loan applications, or allowing your credit report to be pulled, to a two-week period to lessen the impact on your credit score.

Know your all-in costs. A home loan refinance can trigger a bunch of fees: application fees, the cost of an appraisal, origination fees, a document processing fee, an underwriting fee, a credit report charge, title research and insurance, recording fees, tax transfer fees and points, to name several.

But remember, you'll get a clear estimate of mortgage loan fees from each lender you consider.

And don't jump blindly for a "no-cost refinance" pitch. This means the lender is moving the upfront fees to your ongoing costs for the loan, in the form of a higher interest rate — or a greater loan balance.

Gather paperwork. This can be a bit harder these days because so many of us do our financial business online.

But you'll have to gather, print or download statements, pay stubs, and whatever else the lender will need during the loan process.

Lock your rate. You'll have to decide whether or not, and when, to lock in your mortgage refinance rate with the lender, so the rate you're offered for your new loan can't change during a specified period prior to closing.

For the logically minded, it's a hand-wringer — more art than science.

Have cash on hand. There are likely to be property taxes and insurance, closing costs and other expenses to pay at closing, so be sure to set aside enough to cover them.

Again, it's listed in your loan estimate, so there should be no surprises. In some cases, these costs can be added to the mortgage balance, which, on the one hand, limits your upfront costs but, on the other, increases what you owe on your home.

Final tips

If you owe more than your home is worth, you may want to consider whether a government-sponsored mortgage program can be a part of your refinance solution.

These programs come and go — and change names from time to time — but they generally allow homeowners to refinance their mortgage no matter how little equity they have in their home.

And for any refinance, be sure to consider how long it will take for you to recoup the fees and expenses.

But refinancing — for the right reason, with a good rate and a suitable term — can enhance your financial position.

PAY OFF OR REDUCE DEBT

Are you swimming in debt and don't know how you're ever going to pay it off?

You're not alone. In fact, the average U.S. household has nearly $17,000 in credit card debt, according to a 2016 NerdWallet analysis.

1. Create a budget. "The first step to solving your debt problem is to establish a budget," writes former U.S. News contributor David Bakke.

You can use personal finance tools like Mint.com, or make your own Excel spreadsheet that includes your monthly income and expenses.

Then scrutinize those budget categories to see where you can cut costs. "If you don't scale back your spending, you'll dig yourself into a deeper hole," Bakke warns.

2. Pay off the most expensive debt first. Sort your credit card interest rates from highest to lowest, then tackle the card with the highest rate first.

"By paying off the balance with the highest interest first, you increase your payment on the credit card with the highest annual percentage rate while continuing to make the minimum payment on the rest of your credit cards," writes former My Money contributor Hitha Herzog.

3. Pay more than the minimum balance. To make a dent in your debt, you need to pay more than the minimum balance on your credit card statements each month. "Paying the minimum – usually 2 to 3 percent of the outstanding balance – only prolongs a debt payoff strategy," Herzog writes. "Strengthen your commitment to pay everything off by making weekly, instead of monthly, payments." Or if your minimum payment is $100, try doubling it and paying off $200 or more.

4. Take advantage of balance transfers. If you have a high-interest card with a balance that you're confident you can pay off in a few months, Trent Hamm, founder of TheSimpleDollar.com, recommends moving the debt to a card that offers a zero-interest balance transfer.

"You'll need to pay off the debt before the balance transfer expires, or else you're often hit with a much higher interest rate," he warns. "If you do it carefully, you can save hundreds on interest this way."

5. Halt your credit card spending. Want to stop accumulating debt? Remove all credit cards from your wallet, and leave them at home when you go shopping, advises WiseBread contributor Sabah Karimi.

"Even if you earn cash back or other rewards with credit card purchases, stop spending with your credit cards until you have your finances under control," she writes.

6. Put work bonuses toward debt. If you receive a job bonus around the holidays or during the year, allocate that money toward your debt payoff plan.

"Avoid the temptation to spend that bonus on a vacation or other luxury purchase," Karimi writes. It's more important to fix your financial situation than own the latest designer bag.

7. Delete credit card information from online stores. If you do a lot of online shopping at one retailer, you may have stored your credit card information on the site to make the checkout process easier.

But that also makes it easier to charge items you don't need. So clear that information. "If you're paying for a recurring service, use a debit card issued from a major credit card service linked to your checking account," Hamm writes.

8. Sell unwanted gifts and household items. Have any birthday gifts or old wedding presents collecting dust in your closet?

Search through your home, and look for items you can sell on eBay or Craigslist. "Do some research to make sure you list these items at a fair and reasonable price," Karimi writes.

"Take quality photos, and write an attention-grabbing headline and description to sell the item as quickly as possible." Any profits from sales should go toward your debt.

9. Change your habits. "Your daily habits and routines are the reason you got into this mess," Hamm writes. "Spend some time thinking about how you spend money each day, each week and each month."

Do you really need your daily latte? Can you bring your lunch to work instead of buying it four times a week?

Ask yourself: What can I change without sacrificing my lifestyle too much?

10. Reward yourself when you reach milestones. You won't pay down your debt any faster if you view it as a form of punishment.

So reward yourself when you reach debt payoff goals. "The only way to completely pay off your credit card debt is to keep at it, and to do that, you must keep yourself motivated," Bakke writes.

Just make sure to reward yourself within reason.

For example, instead of a weeklong vacation, plan a weekend camping trip. "If you aim to reduce your credit card debt from $10,000 to $5,000 in two months," Bakke writes, "give yourself more than a pat on the back when you do it."

INVEST IN A BUSINESS

Why invest in businesses?

Beyond the potential profits that may come from investing in a portfolio of businesses, investors can enjoy a few additional benefits of buying into businesses they believe in.

First, it's a chance to be a part of the next big thing – to be like the dragons on Dragon's Den and pick exciting businesses, follow their progress as they grow and get credit and recognition for having been one of the first people to spot them.

Second, you get to contribute to the culture of innovation by supporting entrepreneurs when they need it most and giving them a chance to get great new businesses off the ground.

Third, it's a way to get involved with innovation in an area you're interested in or are passionate about, and share in the success of the business.

And, it is the opportunity to support your friends and family on their exciting new business endeavour.

What are you investing in?

Investing in businesses (equity crowdfunding) is about picking early-stage and growth-focused businesses that you think have the potential to grow.

You invest money in them in exchange for a portion of their equity, meaning that you buy shares in their business. If a business that you've invested in succeeds, the shares that you own will become worth more than what you paid for them, and you may be able to sell them at a profit or receive dividend payments in the future.

However, if the business fails – as many businesses do – you will lose some or all of your investment.

What are the main risks of investing in businesses?

There are three broad types of risks when investing in early-stage and growth-focused businesses.

The first is that the business will simply fail – or even that it will tick along without ever really succeeding – and you won't get any of your money back.

The second is that even if the business succeeds, your investment is likely to be illiquid. Even a successful investment will be locked in for a long time – often several years – while the business grows.

This means that you are unlikely to be able to sell the shares, and you will likely not receive dividends, in the early years of your investment no matter how successful it later turns out to be.

Finally, there is the risk of dilution. If the business raises more capital later on (which most successful startups need to do), the percentage of equity that you hold in it will decrease relative to what you originally had.

Dilution in itself is not always a bad thing, and this blog post explains why it is often to be welcomed, but it is something of which you should be aware.

Read our Risk Warning for additional information about the risks associated with investing in early-stage and growth-focused businesses.

The importance of diversification

The key to investing in early-stage and growth-focused businesses successfully – and mitigating the risks described above – is diversification.

Most businesses fail, but the few that do succeed can do so to such a degree that they more than make up for losses.

This means that in order to achieve strong returns, you need to have invested in a few of the big winners.

Your chances of doing so are much greater if you build a diversified portfolio by investing small amounts in many businesses rather than large amounts in just a few. And when we say many, we mean many.

We believe that an effective portfolio should include at least 50 early-stage and growth-focused businesses and potentially 100 or more (there is even data out there to suggest that investing in as many as 800 companies may greatly increase your performance).

One of the main reasons we developed Seedrs was to make it easy to create a diversified portfolio of investments you choose.

By setting the investment minimum very low, we make it possible to invest in many businesses – no matter how much money you are prepared to invest.

Earning returns

The main way you can make money from your investments is by selling your shares in the businesses for more than you paid for them.

There is no active secondary market for shares in private businesses, meaning that you won't be able to sell them immediately.

However, if the company grows to the point where it floats on a stock exchange, is bought by another company or conducts a share buyback, you are likely to be able to sell your shares – often at a significant profit – at that stage.

Alternatively, some businesses may begin paying dividends. T

his can occur if the business has achieved profitability but does not expect to continue growing significantly; it can also happen in cases such as theatre productions or films, where the company has a limited duration and distributes any profits at the end.

SELL AN EBOOK ONLINE

Do you like the idea of selling ebooks online?

Many people do, and it's the ideal lifestyle for a business online. Just imagine... no inventory to store, unlimited supply, instant downloading (no shipping anything off), and high profit margins.

With all of these benefits, it's no wonder why people are jumping on the ebook train to make money online.

But you should know that selling ebooks online isn't a cake walk. You have to invest in advertising, do a lot of free advertising, and be willing to invest hours into marketing your ebook around the web.

Now obviously if you have a large advertising budget, you can pretty much let your website run itself.

With paid advertising, you can get tons of qualified hits to your website, and hopefully get them to buy from you.

But after you get the traffic to your site, it's your job to convert them into customers.

There are many ways to do this, and depending on your price, you will want to test different approaches.

To create an ebook, it's very easy. You can write up a 50-page book in Microsoft Word, convert it into "PDF" format online (pdfonline), price it at around $7 to $19, and upload it to your website for sale.

Now you will have to create a sales description page to promote your product, and this takes a bit of copywriting skills.

But it's nothing you should be worried about. As long as you have a "swipe file", you're good to go.

Selling ebooks online can be a big money-maker. You can earn money on the frontend, and earn tons of cash on the backend sales that you get from your existing and recurring customers.

This is where 80% of your total business profits will come from. So backend marketing is a big reason why you should sell ebooks of your own.

If you sell affiliate products from a site like Clickbank, you can earn money on the frontend, but if you don't get the customer name, how will you get sales from the customer on the backend?

The only way around this (to my knowledge) is to sign up to one of those web hosting affiliate programs (for example), and earn money month after month - for the duration that the customer is enrolled in the web hosting services.

Affiliate marketing and selling affiliate products is a different story, but let me continue on with selling ebooks and digital products of your own.

It's a great lifestyle. You can be out on the beach all while you make money online. You could be sleeping all while you make money with your product.

You could take a vacation and just sit back and watch how your sales and profits increase automatically without your intervention.

It's an amazing business to enter into, but you will have to know a bit about internet marketing to make it successful.

The phrase "Build it and they will come" is non-negotiable online. You have to drive people to your site everyday, and be proactive with your approach.

Take these tips and use them to earn money with selling your own ebook today. It's incredibly easy, and once you learn the ropes, you'll b earning money with your ebook in no time at all.

So, you have successfully created ebooks that contain compelling and useful content. The next thing that you need to do to convert your creations to dollars is to sell them online. Here's how you can do that:

1. Pay per Click advertising. Create ads around keywords where your eBook content was based on. Make your ads easy to understand, powerful, and enticing.

Use words that target human emotions and those terms that can evoke action. Bid higher compare to your competitors so your ads will show on top of the search page results each time your targeted keywords are used by online users.

You will be billed by the search engines each time your ads are clicked. Charge will be based on your bid.

2. Article marketing. This is by far the best methods to use when selling your ebooks. Obviously, your potential clients would like to know if you have what it takes to offer them the kind of information that they are looking for.

There is no better way to do that than sharing a slice of your expertise through your articles.

3. Affiliate marketing. Contact affiliate marketers to help you sell your ebooks online. As these people are equipped with the most effective and newest marketing tools, you can be assured that they can help you boost your sales by up to a hundredfold.

You will share with them a fraction of your revenue each time they make a sale.

4. Forum posting. Connect with your target market by building an ongoing communication with them on forums.

Offer answers to their questions and help them solve their pressing issues. Once you have earned their trust, you can go ahead and pitch in your ebooks.

By the way, would you like to get the newbie-friendly insider's secrets to building a stable, thriving business online... year after year.

CREATE A COURSE ON UDEMY

Step 1: Plan Your Course

• Planning your course is the first step on your course creation journey and it's very important to provide yourself with a solid foundation for building the rest of your course.

• Decide what you want to teach. You probably have an idea of what you want to teach, and now it's time to get really specific.

• Identify what you want your users to learn from your course. Determining this now will go a long way in helping you create a great course structure.

• Scope the content of your course to ensure that there is enough content for users to engage with and achieve their objectives.

This is also where you think through how you want to organize your content. Be sure to conclude each section with either a quiz or a summary to sum up what users have learned.

• Break down your course into smaller, bite-sized lectures and describe what they each need to accomplish.

This step is to help you get more detailed about your content, and break it down into individual sections and lectures.

Write a lecture description for each lecture, summarizing what users will learn.

Step 2: Produce Your Course

This is the most important part of your course creation process.

• As you're creating your lectures, consider different types of learners. Video lectures should alternate between the different lecture types and also between presentation styles such as "talking head", slides, screencasts and drawing boards.

Upload your promotional video so that users can preview your course.

• Include practice activities throughout the course to keep learners engaged—at least one per section. These can take many different forms depending on the content, but may include quizzes, case studies or projects.

• Use the bulk uploader to upload your videos into your course. You can also use the uploader to upload any other resources you're including (supplemental resources, PDF, audio, or presentation lectures).

Once your videos are uploaded, go through your outline and associate the videos with the correct lecture.

Step 3: Polish Your Course
   This step involves making your course ready for publishing.

• Craft a compelling course summary

• Take another look at your course title, and add in a subtitle.

• Create a course image that meets our guidelines.

Step 4: Publish Your Course

• Admins: You are ready to publish your course!

• Non-admins: you will need to submit the course for review and an admin will need to approve it for publishing.

CREATE AN APP

Like so many before you, you have a great app idea burring in your brain, and you have no idea how to bring it and all of its profit potential to fruition.

And like those who have paved the way for app entrepreneurs, you need to learn the ropes.

While some will advise you to hire a developer and invest a fortune in your idea, realists will tell you the risk is too big.

There are tons of app building programs out there that can help you make your vision a reality, but the simple truth is with some planning and methodical work on your part, the process is fairly simple.

We've come up with a three-part guide that will walk you through the steps of profiting from your big idea. Let's start at the very beginning of how to create an app...

• Set a Goal.

Step away from any form of technology and get out a pen and paper and define what it is you want to accomplish.

The starting line in the app development word is a pen and paper, not complex coding and designing. **Ask and answer the following**

questions:

What exactly do you want your app to do?

How are you going to make it appeal to users?

What problem is it going to solve?

How will it simplify life for people?

How will you market your app?

You will not survive in any business if you don't have well defined, clearly set goals! A lack of vision will frustrate you and anyone who you employ to work for you.

Before you do anything, create a clear picture of what you want done!

• Sketch your Ideas.

No! You still cannot turn on your computer.

Now you need to use the pen and paper that has the answers to the questions about your apps purpose to develop a sketch of what it will look like.

Here you move your clearly worded ideas into visual representations of your thoughts. Decide if you are going to give your app away and offer ads to generate money, or are you going to offer it as a paid download.

You can also choose the option to offer in app purchases. If that is something you are going to do, make sure you sketch out those ideas as well.

• Research, research, and then research some more.

Now you can turn your computer on, but not to start blindly designing your app. The leg work is nowhere near done.

You have to dig deep and research the competition of your app idea. I know you think you have one of a kind idea, but the numbers are not in your favor—odds are someone has already tried it. You can look at this in two different ways.

One you can become deflated and give up, or two, you can examine the competition and make your app better.

I prefer the latter. Read the competition's reviews. What did people like/dislike about the app?

Then, use that information to your advantage. Refer back to your pen and paper from steps one and two, and modify and adjust your idea accordingly.

After reading and modifying, your research needs to shift focus a bit. It's time to harness the power of the Internet.

Is your app a truly feasible idea?

Here's where you will examine copyright restrictions and possible technical holds ups. This step is crucial because it will save you money in the long run.

You can't move forward and spend time on an idea that won't work.

Figure out any glitches, and find ways around them, (notice I didn't say give up—"an ounce of prevention..") so you don't have to back track.

Next, shift your research focus to sales and marketing. Reflect back to your sketch about how you are going to make money with your app.

Are you going to stick with your original idea, or are you going to change it? What is your niche? Are you marketing to teens, parents, children, teachers, travelers, gamers?

Determine that target audience right away. It will help you narrow down design ideas.

After you've exhausted your foresight skills, you can begin the fun stuff. Start to look for design ideas. 99design is a great showcase for examining new and innovative design ideas.

Browse through and see what fits your fancy. Keep your target audience in mind when examining designs. A visual appeal is crucial to your final product.

• Wireframe

In the technology world, a wireframe is a glorified story board. Here is where you take your sketch and your design idea, and you give your idea a little more clarity and functionality.

This will become the foundation for your apps development, so it really is a crucial step.

There are stacks of wireframing websites that you can use to help you bring your sketches to digital life with functionality like click through and icons.

The trick is finding one that you like and that is easy for you to use.

• Start Defining the Back End of Your App

We left off with your wireframe, so at this point in your app development, you have a storyboard of how you want your app to function.

Now it's time to use that storyboard to start examine functionality.

Using your wireframe, you need to delineate your servers, APIs, and data diagrams. There are some great do-it-yourself app builders that can provide you with the tools to easily do this.

Some of them even do if for you. If you are unclear of what this technical jargon means, you should probably use a service that provides hosting and a means of collecting data about your app usage.

Regardless of what method you choose to use to develop your app, it is imperative that clear diagrams are created as they will serve as the directions for everyone working on your project.

Should you run across any technical difficulties, you should revise your wireframe to reflect any changes.

• Check Your Model

Here's where you need to call in the troops. Show your demo to friends, family, and anyone else who is willing to give you constructive criticism.

Don't waste your time with people who will tell you, "Wow, that's neat." Seek out those cynics and critics. Brutal honesty is crucial at this phase.

Don't be afraid to look over their shoulder as they are checking out your demo to watch how they navigate things.

If you need to revise any of the layouts or navigation paths, do so. Keep your users in mind, and try to follow their thinking, not your own.

Your end goal with this step is to finalize your apps structure and foundation. You need to have the brains of your app working before you start adding design to avoid frustration later in the process.

• Get Building

With the foundation in place, you can start to put the puzzle together to building your app.

First, your developer will set up your servers, databases, and APIs. If you are using a quality do-it-yourself app builder, this will be done for you.

Do not forget to reflect on the feedback you got from your testers. Modify the apps functionality to reflect any changes you made based on your first phase of testing.

At this point, it's time to sign up for the stores. You need to create an account with Google Play and Apple so that you can get your app on the market.

It may take a few days to go through the process, so don't procrastinate this step.
• Design the Look

Now its time to employ the designers to create your UI, user interface. The user interface is a very important part of your app because people are attracted to how things look and how easy they are to navigate.

Through the design process, you need to keep the feedback you got from your testers in mind, and you need to make sure the design and the navigation reflect the feedback you got. How to design your app?

If you've hired a graphic designer for your app, you will need to get high resolution skins, or visually appealing screens based on your wireframe, for your app.

If you are using a WYSIWYG editor, you need to pick your template and layout for your screens yourself.

I'll stress again, keep that testing feedback in mind when developing the look of your app. You are building for users, not for you!

• Test Your App, AGAIN

A second round of testing is imperative. In this round, you will have both a functioning app as well as a user interface to test.

All the screens of your app should properly work at this point, and your app should be visually appealing as well.

You need to run a battery of tests on your app in its completed form to assure that both the look and the feel of the app meet your expectations.

Proto.io and Pixate are great platforms for testing your app. Both of these programs will allow you to add clickable links to navigate your app.

They will help you examine the final layers, interactions, and design of your app as well. You can use the information you get from this testing phase to help you move forward.

You may be scratching your head and asking, "Didn't I do this with my wireframe?" The answer is, "Well, kind of."

While this may seem similar to your wireframe, it's a lot more detailed. Your wireframe was just the skeleton of your app.

At this point, your app should be both aesthetically pleasing as well as functioning.

• Modify and Adjust

You've taken your prototype for a spin, and you've learned that there are still a few tweaks you need to make.

Now that you've seen your app in it's fully functioning form, you need to call the troops back and ask they to do the same.

Ask the same people who viewed your app in it's development phase to examine it in it's testing phase as well.

Again, open yourself up to constructive criticism, and use the feedback accordingly. Lastly, ask your developer and your designer to make any changes that you feel would be valuable to your app.

• Beta Testing

You've looked at your app through several different lenses, and you think you've managed to develop a smoothly functioning, aesthetically pleasing, problem solving app.

Now, you need to examine how your app is going to function in a live environment.

Android makes this process simple, while iOS likes to keep things in a controlled environment.

There's pros and cons to both approaches, but the bottom line is you need to jump through one last hoop.

You can simply upload your app file on any android device and test it in a live environment. From here on out in your Android app development process, you can monitor your apps progress from your device.

iOS requires you use a platform called TestFlight to beta test your app. Apple is pretty thorough with its directions and instructions for using its beta test platform.

A great feature to this beta testing option is that you can invite testers to review your app before taking it live. It's yet another user lens through which you can view your app.

· Release Your App

You've made it to the finish line. You've brought your idea to fruition, and the last step is to share it with the world.

Hopefully, you've gone on to solve a major problem. If not, with any luck your app has some features that can simplify or bring enjoyment to someone's life.

Regardless, you've accomplished something big. Now it's time to distribute it!

Android and iOS, again are very different with regard to marketing apps.

If you stick with this business, you will see a pattern emerge—Android is a little less strict.

Again, there are pros and cons to both approaches, but as an app entrepreneur, you will need to learn the rules for both.

You can simply add your app to the android store. It will not be reviewed right away. You will instantly be selling your app in the Google Play store.

iOS, on the other hand, will review your app before it can go live. While there is no set time frame for the Apple team to review your app and push it on the shelves, you can guestimate about a week of waiting.

APP STORE

If you are anxious about getting your app onto the devices of users, you can also publish it in Pre-Apps.

This is a great opportunity to have your app viewed by people who like to have a first look at new ideas.

Keep in mind, these people are always reviewing up and coming ideas, so their feedback could be great for you.

They are familiar with #trendingapps, so I'd advise taking this extra step—if for nothing more than to learn more about the app world.

AFFILIATE MARKETING

The lure of affiliate marketing is undeniable; who can resist passive income?

But to make that passive income happen, you have got to put in some work first. To succeed in affiliate marketing, there are a number of crucial steps you must take before you earn that first affiliate profits.

And these steps are, well ... not passive.

The good news is that if you're determined to make this work and are willing to put in the time and effort, you're already well on your way to affiliate marketing success.

All the work you put in is to help you make your first affiliate marketing sale. There is nothing like a first sale to motivate you and make you keep at it.

So, what do you need to do to get started?

Steps to Earning Your First Affiliate Commission

We've broken down the process into seven steps for affiliate marketing beginners.

Following this guide will set you on the right course and have you earning your first commission in no time.

1. Choose a Niche

Before you even begin building your first site, you'll need to decide which niche you're going to target.

Obviously, if you don't know what your site is about or who you're going to target with it, you can't really build a site around it...can you?

If you've already figured this one out, way to go! This is undoubtedly one of the most difficult and overwhelming steps.

If you don't quite know what your niche is yet, here's some advice that you might find useful.

Some key questions to ask yourself when determining your niche are:

What topics am I already passionate about?

It's much easier to work on something if you're passionate about it. Plus, when you have a passion, you're usually quite knowledgeable about it too, so that definitely helps.

For example if you have a passion about about makeup, your niche of choice might be makeup related, too.

Is there money in this niche?

While following your passion is definitely the recommended option, sometimes the possibility of making money in a profitable niche trumps passion.

So, you might not necessarily know much about your niche, but if it's likely to make you money, you can always learn more about it, right?

For example, KitchenFaucetDivas is clearly a site that was built for profit, not passion. Unless of course there is someone out there with a serious passion for kitchen faucets! ;-)

What topic could I see myself easily writing 25, 50, or 100 blog posts about?

The topic you choose must have enough depth that you can create a lot of content for it.

This is important for building an authoritative site, for search engine optimization, and most importantly, for the end user.

If you don't have enough content about a topic, you're not going to be taken very seriously as an authority on the topic and it's unlikely you can convince someone to make a purchase from you.

MoneySavingExpert is a great example of a site with a topic for which you would have a never ending supply of content ideas.

Is there room in this niche for another affiliate marketer?

There are several profitable niches that are also very popular among affiliate markets (e.g., weight loss).

Before jumping on board with a hugely popular niche, make sure there's enough room for you. That is — will you be able to make money and compete with already established marketers? If not, keep looking.

Is there enough interest in/demand for products in this niche?

The niche you choose might draw enough interest from your audience when it comes to reading and acquiring knowledge, but are they willing to buy relevant products too?

Without consumer interest in products, your niche isn't going to make you much money.

Are there affiliate programs available in this niche?

This is obviously a crucial factor to consider. You might come up with an idea for a niche you know a lot about, but are there affiliate programs for the niche?

No affiliate program = no sales. Time to look for a different niche.

2. Research Affiliate Programs

Once you've decided on a niche, it's time to find out what's out there in terms of programs and products to promote.

You've probably already done a bit of research for this while researching your niche — now you need to dig deeper.

Choosing an affiliate program will take some work, but don't be afraid to invest a significant amount of time into it because this is, of course, where your income will come from.

Choosing the right program will make it well worth your while!

When choosing an affiliate program, keep these key points in mind:

What type of merchants use the program/ affiliate network?

You want to make sure other similar sellers are also using the network, as this can help you gauge your likelihood of success with the particular program.

How much commission are you likely to make from the products?

Make sure you sign up for programs that are profitable and generate a sufficient return in on investment. Some tips:

If using ClickBank, products should have over a 50% commission (preferably 60%), and have a high gravity rating (meaning they're in demand).

For CPA (cost-per-action) programs, commissions should be over $1, and products shouldn't be overly restrictive in how you can promote them.

For physical products, look for commissions over $40.

Do you want to be associated with the products and services?

The products and services you will be promoting to your audience must be relevant and good quality.

Make sure you believe in them and know everything about them, because this will be crucial to you delivering the sales pitch to your audience.

You need to build trust with your audience so make sure the products and services you choose to promote are trustworthy enough.

Ads like the one below often lead to sketchy products — do you want to be associated with a product that promises results that may or may not be true?

What kind of support does the program provide?

Be sure to check what kind of customer support you can expect from your affiliate program once you have signed up.

Do your research online and if possible, speak to other sellers using the program to get their thoughts.

Can you speak to someone via phone or Skype or do you have to wait 72 hours for email responses? Be clear on this because trust me, you will need support at one point or another.

3. Build a Site

Steps 1 and 2 are all about research and figuring out what's possible and profitable. Now, it's time to start putting your research into action.

Assuming you don't already have a website built, this will be the next step. Fortunately, building a site isn't as complicated or labor-intensive as it was in the past.

If you're a newbie to building sites, the easiest way to set up a site is by using WordPress.

The WordPress CMS is very easy to use and while coding skills can come in handy, for the most part you will not require any tech knowledge to set up your site.

You need to follow a few steps to have your site up and running:

• Buy a domain.

Your domain is the address for your website (e.g., www.affilorama.com) so this is the first thing you will need to do when setting up your site.

Considering there are millions of websites on the internet, it's possible that the domain name you want may already be taken by someone else.

So make sure you have several options in mind. Be sure to read our advice on how to choose a good domain name.

• Purchase and set up hosting.

If your domain is your address, hosting is like the actual house within which your site will live. It's your own little slice of the internet — the place where all your website files live.

Hosting is very affordable these days, so don't unnecessarily scrimp on costs. Go with a reputable, reliable provider because your affiliate marketing business depends on it.

• Install WordPress.

Once your hosting is set up, you need to install a content management system (CMS) for your site.

We recommend WordPress because it is easy to use and a beginner (like you!) can quite quickly figure out how it works.

Most good hosting providers will have a one-click install option for WordPress, which means it will only take you a couple of minutes and you will have WordPress installed on your site.

• Install your theme.

A WordPress theme provides all the styling of a site that you (and your audience) see on the front end.

There are thousands of themes available, so choosing one might seem daunting at start. **Our advice:** go with something simple and easy to customize. You can always change it later.

The AffiloTheme is a great option. Completely customizable, and built specifically for affiliate marketers, you can use this WordPress theme to bypass much of the initial learning curve other affiliate marketers will experience.

You can also search for themes on a site like Theme Forest.

Create content.

Finally, once your site is ready, it's time to create content for it. The content you create must be relevant to your niche but also interesting and engaging enough to keep your audience coming back.

You should also ensure the site content is search engine-friendly. More details about content creation in Step 4.

4. Produce Excellent Content

Now that your site is set up and you've joined an affiliate program, you're ready to begin perhaps the most time-consuming (but potentially rewarding) part of the affiliate business: Producing content.

This is where the overused but truer-than-ever phrase "content is king" comes into play.

Your goal for your site will be to establish it as an authority site in your niche, and the main way to do this is to consistently produce unique, high-quality content.

This could consist of:

• Product reviews.

Your affiliate site model could be based off writing reviews about different products or services.

This is a common model and if done well, can prove very useful in generating affiliate income.

For example, The Wire Cutter is focused on writing reviews of several different kinds of products and helping their readers make the best decision about the product they want to buy.

After reading a review on their site, if the user clicks through to the product/service using the affiliate link, The Wire Cutter will earn a commission from.

Blog posts that address common problems, questions or issues relevant to your target market.

Creating blog content is a very useful and effective way of consistently building content on a site.

When creating blog posts, it's a good idea to do some keyword research to figure out what it is that your audience is interested in and searching for online.

Also, be sure to research competitors, forums and social media to narrow down on topics for your blog.

For example, Security Guard Training HQ has a very extensive blog on a variety of topics relevant for anyone interested in security guard training, jobs and more.

• Evergreen content.

If you are building a site that has the potential for information that will never age and remain useful for your audience, you have the opportunity to create what is known as evergreen content.

It's important to carry out extensive keyword research before planning any evergreen content for a site like this, as your site could hugely benefit from the proper usage of keywords within such content.

For example, the content on Super Weddings is useful whether you're organizing a wedding today or next year.

All the content on the site is created accordingly. To make things easier for the audience, it is separated into categories to make it very convenient for the reader to find what they're looking for.

This, of course, is also very good for SEO.

• Informational products.

Giving away a free informational product such as an e-book, an email series or a mini-course is a popular tactic many affiliate marketers use.

Usually, your readers will have to provide their email addresses to receive the product from you. You can then use this to sell to them via email marketing.

Additionally, an informational product can generate interest in the actual product you're trying to sell.

If your product is popular enough and brings enough traffic to your site, you could also monetize the traffic in other ways, such as AdSense.

A good example is DatingMetrics, where you're tempted with a Free Texting Crash Course in exchange for your email.

The real marketing will begin once the user has downloaded this course.

The type of content you create for your website will largely depend on your niche, as certain types of content perform better in some niches than others.

Remember: Purchasing generic content is NOT an effective method to build your site. While it may be tempting to populate your site this way, in the long run it won't help you to position yourself as an expert in your niche (and ultimately means less traffic and fewer sales).

5. Build an Audience

Building an audience for your site will, in some ways, follow naturally once you start producing excellent content.

An interested audience will not only bring you consistent traffic, but also result in consistent sales for you.

So how do you start building an audience for a completely new site? Here are some ideas:

• Promote your content via social media.

The easiest and most common way to start building an audience for a website is via social media.

Depending on your niche and industry, you can choose from Facebook, Twitter, Instagram, Pinterest and several other niche and location-specific networks.

Building up an engaged and interested following on social media is a great opportunity to build relationships and once you have their trust, promote your products and services to them.

I'll use MoneySavingExpert.com as an example again. The site has over 154,000 likes on its Facebook page and it connects with the audience by sharing links to content but also asking money-saving/budgeting related questions.

The highly engaged readers then visit the website, where they read content and no doubt make purchases.

• Guest post on high-traffic blogs.

While your site is still new, it's a good idea to start capitalizing on someone else's audience. Continue focusing on building your own content, but also considering writing content for a few big, high-traffic blogs that are relevant for your niche.

By writing content for a bigger site, you are able to get in front of another audience and showcase your expertise on a particular topic. This will eventually lead to more traffic to your site, as well.

• Build an email list.

Let no one tell you that email marketing is dead. An email list is crucial for every affiliate marketer.

You can start building up your email list with a lead magnet (like the information products mentioned previously) or even just by encouraging your audience to sign up for your updates.

You can then push your content to this audience via email and also direct them to your affiliate offers.

Don't be sleazy about the sales, but if you build up enough trust with your email audience; when the time comes, they will not mind purchasing a product from you.

• Use basic SEO techniques to increase search engine traffic to your site.

Organic search remains an important source of traffic for any website, so it's important that you optimize your website for search engines as well.

When creating your content, you must always do so keeping the reader in mind first, but don't forget to follow a few basic SEO principles as well.

Learn SEO yourself or hire a good SEO marketer to help you maximize on-page and off-page SEO opportunities for your site.

If your site starts to appear in search results for terms relevant to your niche, it will be a huge boost towards building your audience (and your sales)!

• Invest in paid advertising.

Many affiliate marketers use paid advertising to generate additional traffic to their site and drive more sales.

Paid advertising on social media is often a good place to start, as these networks tend to be more affordable.

You may also want to consider taking out inexpensive banner ads on small niche sites. Depending on your niche, Google AdWords could also be a good option to drive some paid traffic to your site.

6. Promote Affiliate Offers

Finally, the part we've all been waiting for!

This, my friends, is where things really kick into high gear. Many fly-by-night affiliates will jump right to this step and bypass steps 1–5 completely.

And this is what will set you apart.

Once you've shown that you can offer something of value in your niche, it's time to continue adding value by promoting products that will be useful and helpful for your audience.

You can promote your offers in a number of ways. It will depend on the type of site you've built and also what you're selling. **Some ideas include:**

- Product reviews.

Write honest, real reviews about products. Build up trust with your audience, and remember that they rely on your opinion.

Don't just point out all the positives of a product and gloss over the negatives. An honest opinion will be valued.

Add compelling images and make mention of useful features, specifications and other details.

Your product review can then link to the page (with your affiliate ID attached), where your audience can make a purchase if they're interested. If do, hooray! You've made your first sale.

• Banner ads.

You can put up banners on your site, to promote your affiliate offers. Most affiliate programs will usually provide their own creatives when you sign up for their offers.

All you have to do is insert the banner on a highly trafficked page (your affiliate tracking is usually embedded within the code). Banner ads in the right locations can do a great job of driving sales.

Below are some examples of banners that Templatic provides to its affiliates.

In-text content links.

This is a very common way to promote offers. For example, you will often see a blog post with links to certain products or services.

If the reader clicks through and makes a purchase, the blog owner will make a commission.

These in-text links blend in with other content on your site and are a great way of promoting an offer within your content, without being over-the-top salesy with banners.

Email promotions.

If you have built up an email list, you could also promote your affiliate offers via email promotions.

Just make sure you build up a relationship with your audience first instead of going for the hard sell straightaway. The emails you send out must contain your affiliate links to products so when your audience click through. the sale is attributed to you.
- Discounts and giveaways.

Many affiliate programs will often run promotions with good discounts or giveaways that might be attractive to your audience.

For example, if you're an Amazon Associate and the site have a big Holiday Sale, it would be the perfect opportunity for you to promote discounts to your website visitors.

This is a great way to promote your offers while also providing good value to your audience.

When promoting affiliate offers, just make sure you are fully aware of all the terms and conditions attached to your affiliate program.

Some programs can be strict about how they allow you to promote their products. For example, some may limit you to banner ads and links only, while others will allow you to use paid advertising, but won't allow email marketing.

Also, make sure you have a disclaimer on your website that advises your audience that you may have links that promote affiliate offers.

This is necessary for several affiliate programs and also a basic courtesy to your website visitors. In the U.S., the FTC mandates disclosure for affiliate marketers (and anyone issuing endorsements), as well.

7. Rinse, Lather, and Repeat

Now that you're done with Steps 1 - 6, Step 7 is simply to keep doing what you're doing. Yes, seriously!

Your ongoing work as an affiliate marketer will be to repeat steps 4 - 6 on a continual basis.

Building a site up to a point where it can make you consistent income takes a bit of work and you must be willing to constantly create, promote, market, innovate and of course, sell.

NETWORK MARKETING

Many people are scared away from network marketing, also known as multi-level marketing (MLM), because of all the myths and misunderstanding about this type of business.

Part of negativity comes from reported low MLM success rates. However, a multi-level marketing business isn't destined to fail any more than any other business.

Regardless of the home business you start, success comes from doing the work to build it.

For some reason, many people don't view their MLM business as a business, like they would if they opened a franchise or started a business from scratch.

One of the most important things you can do to insure your success is to treat your MLM venture as the business it is.

Here are a few other tips to help you improve your multi-level marketing (MLM) and recruiting efforts within the world of direct selling:

1) Brush Up on the Realities of MLMs

To stay safe from pyramid schemes and MLM scams, arm yourself with knowledge. Learn about the direct sales industry as a whole, research

MLM companies carefully, and determine if you're a good match with your sponsor.

The truth is, while you can get rich in MLM, statistics show that less than one out of 100 MLM representatives actually achieve MLM success or make any money.

However, that's not necessarily the MLM business' fault. Most athletes never make it to the Olympics, but that's not sport's or the Olympics' fault.

Any great feat requires knowledge and action.

2) Find a Company With A Product You Love

Too many people get caught up in the hype of potential big income from MLM, that they don't pay enough attention to what the company is asking you to sell.

You can't sell something or share your business if you don't genuinely have pride in what you are representing.

Do your MLM research and partner with a company that has a product you can get excited about.

Don't forget to look into the company's compensation plan before you join and make sure it is favorable to you.

3) Be Genuine and Ethical

One reason that direct selling gets a bad rap is that many representatives use hype and sometimes deception to lure in new recruits.

This leads many to believe that the MLM companies themselves encourage this behavior, when in truth, they don't.

Legitimate MLM companies want you to be honest in your dealings with customers and potential recruits.

If you love your product, your enthusiasm is enough to promote it. Just make sure you're not over-the-top or making exaggerated or false claims.

Good business conduct will ensure that your customers and recruits don't feel duped, and as a result, will stick with you.

4) Don't Barrage Your Friends and Family

Nothing will annoy your family and cost you friends more than constantly pestering them about your business.

There's nothing wrong with letting them know what you're doing and seeing if they have an interest, but if the answer is "no," let it go.

Many companies suggest making a list of 100 people you know, and while that's not wrong, you should consider that most successful MLMers have very few people from their original list of 100 people in their business. In most cases, friends and family who are in the business often come AFTER seeing the MLMer's success.

Success in MLM comes from treating it like any other business in which you focus on the people who want what you have to offer.

That means deciding who the target market is for your products/services, as well as the business opportunity.

5) Identify Your Target Market

One of the biggest mistakes new MLMers make is looking at everyone (including friends and family #4) as a potential customer or recruit.

This is one area where the MLM industry gets it wrong. Like any other business, you're going to have greater success and efficiency if you identify your target market and focus your marketing efforts at them.

Someone who doesn't care about vitamins or health and wellness isn't a good person to pester about your business.

6) Make an Effort to Share Your Product//Business Plan Everyday

Many MLM sponsors will have you focus on recruiting new business builders; however, your income, in legitimate MLM, comes from the sales of products or services (whether through you or your recruits).

Further, customers who love the products or services can more easily be converted into new business builders.

Just like any other business (home-based or otherwise), getting the word out about your product or service can benefit your target market is the key to generating new customers and recruits.

Some ideas include sharing a product sample, inviting a neighbor to host a product party, or starting a website or social media account.

7) Sponsor, Don't Recruit

One of the benefits of MLM is the ability to bring in new business builders and profit from the sales they make in their business.

While some see this as "using" others, the reality is that you're being rewarded for helping others succeed. But for them to succeed, you need to see your role not as racking up as many recruits as possible, but in being a leader and trainer.

The focus then is on the success of those you help in the business, not on you.

That means you need to take time to train them, answer questions, celebrate their successes, and be a support when things are tough.

8) Set a Goal for Parties or Presentations

MLM is a person-to-person to business. While many people don't like that aspect, especially in the digital age, the reality is that it's the personal touch that sells the products and business, and retains customers and business builders.

Based on your compensation plan and goals, determine how many people you need to show your products or business to reach your goals in the time you want.

Doing so will ensure you grow your business rather than just sustain it.

7) Listen and Sell the Solution

Many companies provide scripts to help you sell the product or service. While these can be helpful in teaching you about your product and dealing with objections, sales is all about being a solution to what a customer needs.

By qualifying your contact first, and then listening to their needs, you can tailor your pitch so that you're the solution to their problem.

8) Learn How to Market

MLMers often stick to the three-foot rule (everyone within 3-feet of you is a prospect) and other traditional marketing tactics.

But direct sales is like any other business. It can and should be marketed in a variety of ways that takes into consideration your target market, what it needs, how you can help it, and where it can be found.

To that end, you can use a variety of marketing tools including a website (check your companies policies about websites), email, and social media to increase product sales and interest in your business.

9) Stand Out from Other Distributors

One of the challenges of MLM is convincing prospects to buy or join with you as opposed to the other reps that live in the neighborhood or they know online.

You're selling the same stuff as thousands of others, meaning consumers have a choice. You need to do something that makes you unique compared to everyone else. Give people a reason to choose you over other reps.

Some options include more personalized service, starting your own rewards program, or something that offers greater value.

10) Develop a System for Following Up

While you don't want to pester and annoy people, in many cases, with good follow up, you can make the sale or recruit at a future time.

Sales is often about timing, and 'no' in sales doesn't always mean 'never.'

If someone tells you no, but there was something in the dialogue that suggested they might be interested in the future, ask if you can put them on your mailing or email list, or if you can call in six months to follow up.

Many will give you their email or phone number just because they want to be nice. Even so, use your calendar or contact system to remind you when to call.

DESIGN T-SHIRTS

Designing your own t-shirt can be a fun, creative activity, and may even bring you some money if you decide to sell your designs.

Whether you intend to print the shirt yourself or send it off to a professional printer, you can still come up with the design for your shirt right at home.

Part 1 Planning Your Design

1. Think about what your design is going to represent. Maybe you are advertising your cleaning company, your rock band, or your favorite sports team.

Maybe you're using a personal illustration. The purpose of the design will determine the design.

If you are advertising a company, band, sporting team, or brand, you will likely need to focus on logo.

The Nike swoosh logo, for example, is a very simple but effective design. A design for a sporting team might feature the team colors or the team's mascot.

A design for your band might focus on an image of the band or a graphic that represents the band's style or sound.

If you are making a t-shirt to showcase a personal illustration or drawing, you will need to focus on how it will look on a t-shirt.

Think about how original the illustration is and how the colors are working in the illustration.

Consider using a photo in your design. Use your own photo. You may use a picture made by someone else, but only if you have acquired the legal rights to use that image. You can also buy a stock image.

2. Pick a color scheme. When designing a t-shirt, its important to think about color contrast.

This means how certain ink colors in the design will appear against a lighter colored shirt or a darker colored shirt.

Certain ink colors look more vibrant on a lighter or darker shirt on the computer screen than they actually do when printed.

When using lighter shirts, avoid pastel colors like yellow, light blue, or light pink. These colors will be visible on the shirts but may not be legible at a distance. And if you are designing a shirt with a logo, you want to make sure that logo is legible from far away!

If you decide to use pastel colors, add an outline of a darker color to the lighter color to highlight the text and make it easier to read.

Darker colored shirts look good with lighter ink colors, such as pastels. But be careful when using darker ink colors on darker colored shirts like cardinal (dark blue), maroon, or forest green.

These colors may look great on the computer or in a drawing, but when they print, the shirt color sometimes distorts the ink color. As a result, they can appear more brown or dull.

If you decide to use Adobe Illustrator to create your design, the Global Colours settings can help immensely with color schemes.

3. Add dimension to the design. Once you've added your colors to the design, it may look good but still a bit flat or one dimensional.

To create more depth to a certain area of the design, add a color that is the shade of the color beneath it. This will brighten up the design and give it some dimension.

- If you plan to use software with a high capacity for manipulation (such as Adobe Photoshop, InDesign, Gimp, Adobe Illustrator, or Paint Shop Pro), you can use a standard image and radically transform it to fit your needs.

- Creating a vector outline on Inkscape is an especially effective way to resize a photo if necessary.

4. Balance your design. This means combining all the parts or elements to form a whole. How you do this depends on the composition of your design.

Maybe your design has a lot of smaller elements, like stars, plants or animals. Or may it is one large design with one main figure or image.

Think about how you can make the design look cohesive, so that all the parts or elements fit well together.

A balanced image will immediately draw the eye in rather than away from an image.

5. Determine the placement of the design on the t-shirt. Would your design work better as a centered image, an image on the top left of the t-shirt or as a wraparound image?

If you are designing a t shirt for a brand or company, a simple design in the center of the shirt may be the most effective.

Don't forget you can also use the back of the t-shirt to include a branding slogan ("Just Do It"). Or a song lyric from a song by the band you are designing the shirt for.

6. Complete a final mock up of the design. It's best to sketch your ideas out before putting them on your t-shirt. Try out several different designs and color combinations. Keep in mind color contrast and dimension. Make sure the image is balanced and cohesive.

When in doubt, get a second opinion. Ask friends, family, or coworkers what design and color scheme they like best.

Part 2. Making a Digital Image of the Design

1. Use Adobe Photoshop to touch up your paper sketches. If your paper sketches are not high quality or drawn with clear lines, this option may not work. If your sketch is high quality:

- Scan the sketches to your computer. Then, retouch them in Photoshop.

- Clean up the lines. Play with the filters, colors, brightness, contrast, saturation, or any other effects at your disposal.

- Add lines, flourishes, splatter effects, and other embellishments that might make the design more dynamic and balanced (where appropriate).

- Make sure that the entire layout is internally consistent by keeping proportions reasonable, styles consistent, and colors cohesive.

2. Use computer software to create the design. If you aren't happy with the quality of your paper sketches, use computer software to draw line art on Photoshop.

If you have a computer drawing tablet, you can color and draw straight onto Photoshop or a similar program.

3.Add text to the design, if desire. Look for a font that complements your overall design, rather than overwhelm it. The font should work with the image(s) in your design to create a balanced design.

- Think about the fonts on some of the more well known logos or designs. The font should relate back to the company or brand's overall style.

Nike's Just Do It's slogan, for example, is in a bold and simple font, just like their bold and simple swoosh logo. In contrast, the font used for a sports team or a garage rock band may be more elaborate or ornate.

- Make sure any filters you are using on the design are also applied to the font. If you are working with layers on Photoshop, you will need to drag your font layers below the photo effects layers.

- Use free fonts from an online site like defont.com. You can also access free brush designs from brusheezy.com.

- Look at how to add fonts to your PC, Illustrator, or Photoshop if necessary.

- If you're feeling adventurous with design, you can make your own.

4. Create a prototype. The easiest way to do this is to print the design and iron it onto a plain shirt.

However, if you want to test the quality of your design, you can hire a printing company to create a professional prototype.

5. Produce the shirt(s). For a small-scale operation, you can continue ironing on the design.

If you'd like to make shirts at a larger scale, however, you can pay a printing company to make them for you.

Part 3. Screen-Printing Your Design

1. Gather your supplies. To screen-print your design at home, you will need:

- A plain t-shirt
  - 50 ml bottle of degreaser (available at your local art store)
  - 1 liter cold water
  - A large brush
  - 500 ml of emulsion
  - A small bottle of sensitizer
  - A bottle of screen printing ink
  - A squeegee or a coating tray
  - A small wooden stick
  - A hair dryer
  - A transparency
  - A printing screen

You can purchase a printing screen at your local art store. Or make your own by buying a mesh screen and a canvas stretcher frame.

Stretch the mesh across the frame and staple the edges down so that the mesh is taut. For standard designs on a light shirt, a 110-195 mesh works best. For fine designs with multiple colors, use a 156-230 mesh.

2. Prepare the printing screen. Mix the degreaser and the cold water together. Place the brush in the mixture and then brush the mixture on to the screen.

Make sure you brush both sides of the screen. You just want to give the screen a light brush so don't worry about putting too much of the mixture on the screen.

Let the screen dry.

3. Mix the emulsion and the sensitizer together. Take 20 ml of water and pour it into the bottle of sensitizer. Mix the sensitizer well by shaking for an about a minute.

• Add the sensitizer into the emulsion.

• Use the small wooden stick to mix the sensitizer and the emulsion together.

• The color of the emulsion should change from blue to green. There should also be small bubbles forming in the emulsion.

• Place the lid loosely back on the emulsion and place it in a dark area or room for an hour. After an hour, check that all the small bubbles in the emulsion have disappeared.

• If they do not disappear after an hour, leave the emulsion to sit for another hour until the bubbles are gone.

4. Apply the emulsion on the screen. In a very dim room or with a low red light, drip a line of photo emulsion across the screen and use a squeegee to spread it around.

The emulsion will leak through the screen, so be sure to squeegee both sides of the screen.

You can also use a coating tray to apply the emulsion to the screen. Do this by placing the screen on a clean towel and tilting it away from you slightly.

Place the coating tray at the bottom of the screen and carefully pour the emulsion on the screen as you move the tray up the screen.

Leave the emulsion to dry in a completely black room for about twenty minutes. Use a fan to help the screen dry.

5. Place the transparency down backward on the screen. Now you're ready to burn your image into the emulsion.

Do this by placing the screen flat, placing the transparency down backward, and placing a piece of glass over the transparency to ensure that it doesn't move.

6. Burn the design into the emulsion. A 500-watt lightbulb will burn the transparency image into the emulsion in roughly fifteen minutes.

The exact times for this process depend on the light and emulsion you use.

Specific directions for the light needed should be on the packaging of the purchased emulsion.

7. Rinse the screen. Let the screen soak in a thin layer of water for about two minutes. Then rinse any excess emulsion off with a hose or in the shower.

8. Place waterproof tape around the edges of the underside of the screen. The flat side of the screen will go facedown on the shirt, and the side with the frame is where you will use the ink.

To make sure no ink ends up leaking around the frame, use waterproof tape to secure around the edges where the screen stretches over the frame.

9. Lay your t-shirt on a flat surface. Make sure there are no wrinkles. Place the screen on top of the t-shirt, where you would like your design to be.

Place the screen on top, making sure that the screen and design are aligned.

Clip your shirt down to a firm piece of cardboard. Doing this will ensure your t-shirt remains flat and unwrinkled. It will also make it easier to move your t-shirt to a safe spot later to dry.

If possible, have a friend hold the screen down tight while you spread the ink.

10. Spread a tablespoon of screen printing ink on the top of the screen. Using your squeegee, coat the screen by spreading the line of ink from top to bottom.

The mesh is actually quite thick, so this step is more of a primer.

Use very light pressure so you don't push any ink through the screen.

11. Squeegee the screen. With the screen flooded, you're ready to transfer the design to the shirt.

Use the squeegee at a 45° angle in both hands to evenly distribute the pressure. If possible, ask a friend to hold the screen in place.

Drag the ink back up across the flooded screen over the design.

12. Cure the ink. Using a hairdryer, apply even heat to the design for several minutes. Cure the ink before using the next screen to add additional layers of the graphic in different colors.

If you use the proper screen-printing technique and cure it, your t-shirt will be washing machine safe.

13. Wash your screen once you are done making your shirts. Use cold water and scrub it with a sponge to get the ink out. Let the screen air dry.

Part 4. Stenciling Your Design

1. Gather your materials. To stencil your design onto a t-shirt, you will need:

• A black and white print out of your design. Its important to use a black and white printout of your design so it will be easy to trace.

• A piece of contact paper, or a transparency

• A craft knife, or exacto knife

• A plain t-shirt

- A piece of cardboard big enough to cover the front area of the shirt

2. Tape the design to a piece of contact paper. Contact paper is clear paper used for covering books. It has a normal side and a sticky side that peels off.

You want to tape your paper to the peeling side so that the design is visible through the front of the contact paper—the non-sticky side.

You can also use a piece of transparency or clear paper. Attach it to the printout of your design with tape.

3. Use a sharp craft knife to cut out the black parts of the design. Lay the attached papers on a flat surface, like a table.

Trace the lines with the craft knife or an exacto knife. Keep in mind the black parts you cut out are the parts of the design that will be filled with paint.

4. Peel the sticky side off the contact paper. Remove the normal paper with the design from the contact paper as well. Place the sticky stencil onto the t-shirt, making sure it is straight and not wrinkled.

If you are using a transparency or clear paper instead of contact paper, attach the transparency to the shirt with tape.

5. Place a piece of cardboard inside the t-shirt. Doing this separates the front and back so the ink doesn't bleed through to the other side.

6. Use a sponge brush to paint on the fabric paint. Only put paint on the spots that have been cut out of the contact paper—the spots that will be painted in dark on the t-shirt.

Let the paint dry. Test the paint by gently touching the painted spots. If paint comes away on your finger, it is not fully dry.

7. Peel the contact paper off of the t-shirt when the paint is dry. You will now have a stenciled on t-shirt.

You can use the stencil to make another shirt if you want more than one stenciled t-shirt.

Part 5. Bleach Painting Your Design

1. Use bleach safely. Bleach painting is a fun, easy, and inexpensive way to create a design on a t-shirt, especially text based designs. But, remember bleach is toxic, so keep it out of reach of children.

Always protect your eyes, clothing, and any open cuts from coming into contact with bleach.

If you have sensitive skin, you should wear thin kitchen gloves while bleach painting.

2. Gather your supplies.

You will need:

• Fabric safe household bleach

• A synthetic bristle paint brush (go for an inexpensive one, as you'll just be bleaching it anyway!)

• A glass or ceramic bowl

• A white towel or rag

- White chalk

- A piece of cardboard

- A dark colored cotton blend shirt

You can try this method on a lighter colored shirt, but the bleach painting will show up better on darker colors.

3. Place your shirt on a flat surface. Then, slide the piece of cardboard inside your shirt. It will act as an even surface as you write your design. It will also stop the bleach from bleeding through the back of your shirt.

4. Use the white chalk to sketch out your design on the shirt. This could be your favorite saying ("Bazinga!" "Reach for the Stars"), the name of your band, or the logo of your brand.

Don't worry if you need the smudge out the chalk lines and re-sketch the design. The chalk lines will wash out once you've completed the bleach painting.

5. Fold the sides of the shirt under the cardboard. Secure the shirt to the cardboard with elastics or small clips. This will keep the cardboard from slipping while you bleach paint.

6. Prepare the bleach. Pour a few cups of the bleach into the glass or ceramic bowl. Use a towel to wipe up any drips. You don't want any drops of bleach to end up on your clothing.

7. Dip your brush into the bleach. Drag it on the edge of the bowl to eliminate any dripping.

8. Use steady strokes to trace the chalk lines of your design. For an even bleach line, reload your brush every two inches. The fabric will quickly soak up the liquid so work quickly, but with a steady hand.

9. Finish tracing your design. Then, take a break to allow the bleach to react with the fabric of the shirt.

Look over the shirt. Are there any uneven spots or light areas? If so, go back in with your bleach filled brush and even out the design.

10. Let the shirt sit in the sun for at least an hour. This will allow the bleach to process and lighten.

Depending on the cotton content of your shirt, the color of your design will range from dark red, to orange, to pink, or even white.

11. Rinse and hand wash your shirt. Hang it to dry. Admire your new permanent bleach design.

Wash the shirt with like colors. The chalk lines should wash out, leaving only the bleach design.

SELL DIGITAL FILES ON ETSY

When Jenny Kun's daughter was born, Jenny designed a few prints to hang in the new nursery.

One night, while browsing Pinterest, she discovered a digital download for sale on Etsy and inspiration struck. 'I uploaded a few products and I was shocked — I got a sale on my first night', Jenny says.

Since opening her Etsy shop, The Crown Prints, in August 2015, Jenny has sold close to 5000 digital downloads of her original art.

Jenny loves that digital downloads let shoppers make a purchase and have new art hanging in their home in minutes. 'As a consumer, I really enjoy that instant gratification', she says.

Jenny also loves that selling digital downloads allows her to run a business without dealing with headaches like shipping.

Shop owners across Etsy who offer digital downloads in their shop are selling everything from sewing patterns to party printables to beautifully designed resumé templates.

Offering digital downloads is one way you can add more listings to your shop and exercise your creativity.

Selling digital downloads can also be a low-maintenance way to stay in touch with your creative and entrepreneurial passions.

Claudine Hellmuth sells printable gift box templates that she illustrates and designs. When she first started selling digital downloads on Etsy in 2011, Claudine was self-employed and had more time to devote to creating new digital designs and marketing her shop.

She recently went back to a full-time job as a graphic designer, but her Etsy shop remains a source of income on the side. 'It's such a great way to create passive income!' Claudine says. 'You don't have to store or ship your product and you can sell the same item multiple times.'

Whether you're thinking about starting a new shop or just want to try something new, these tips will help you get started selling digital items.

Jenny created these animal silhouette prints for her daughter's nursery and they inspired her to try selling digital downloads on Etsy. She's not currently selling these designs, but they'll be added to her shop soon.

Getting Started

Listing a digital download on Etsy is just like creating a listing for a physical product, except you'll upload the file your customers will receive when they make a purchase.

After buyers purchase a digital file on Etsy, it's immediately available on their downloads page. You can upload audio, image or text files to your listing. See all the steps of listing a digital item.

Although no special skills are required to list a digital download on Etsy, a good working knowledge of design programs like Adobe Illustrator will make creating files easier, says Jenny.

'I use Adobe Illustrator because it's a vector-based program that gives me the flexibility to resize my designs', she says. 'Once you get the hang of it, it's a great tool to have in your toolset.'

Remember that a big part of running a business on Etsy is learning and adapting your shop over time.

Claudine recommends experimenting with selling digital downloads by starting with a few designs. 'You don't have to wait to have hundreds of designs to open your shop', she says. 'List a few designs, see what your customers respond to and then make more of whatever category is selling well.'

Tips for Success

If you're already familiar with the process of listing and selling on Etsy, listing your first digital item should feel familiar.

But, there are some nuances to know about when photographing and pricing digital items, and shoppers might have different customer service expectations.

Photographing

In addition to stylized photos of a completed project, Sarah includes a fifth photo to explicitly state that the listing is for a downloadable sewing pattern.

Great photography is essential for any listing on Etsy, but photographing digital items and ensuring that shoppers understand exactly what they're buying poses certain challenges.

Sarah Norwood sells hand-sewn lingerie and digital download lingerie patterns in her shops Ohhh Lulu and Ohhh Lulu Sews.

Sarah includes photos in her listings that communicate the aesthetic of her brand and show shoppers what they can create with her patterns. 'I always try to create a mood with my photos', Sarah says.

'So even if it's just a picture of the pattern itself, I try to give it a romantic feeling or style it in such a way that people can really picture themselves using it.'

Adding a stylized photo of the pattern itself has dramatically cut down on the number of confused customers Sarah encounters who think they're purchasing the finished item and not a pattern. Emphasizing in your titles and tags that the item is a digital download can also help.

Simple props like a vase of flowers and clean marble and wood surfaces are essential to Jenny's home photo setup.

Jenny has also tailored her photography to best capture her downloadable art prints. When she first started selling her prints, she used standard mock-ups, many of which are sold on Etsy, that placed her art into a frame and setting photographed and designed as a separate image.

'I wasn't sure it was showing my products in their best light because a lot of sellers are using the same mock-ups', she says.

Now, she sets up her own frames and props at home and photographs them herself. 'I like doing that because I feel like I have complete control over my branding and my look', she says.

Customer Service

A subtle banner across the bottom on her listing images lets shoppers know that Claudine's product is a printable kit.

Digital products will save you storage space and trips to the post office, but they can sometimes require extra customer service effort.

As a pattern seller, Sarah has found that her communication with pattern customers is much more in-depth than the questions she gets from shoppers who purchase lingerie from her.

'Sometimes customers need more step-by-step instruction, especially if they're new to sewing', she says. 'So I might not spend a lot of time with order management, but I spend a lot of time helping people remotely.'

Sarah uses her blog to share more in-depth details and how-to's with her customers. Creating these resources allows her to reply with a link for more info instead of repeatedly answering the same questions via Convo.

Claudine has also found that shoppers sometimes need some additional resources to make the most of their digital downloads purchase.

On her YouTube channel, she shares videos that show exactly how to put together her printable, 3D gift boxes.

The questions and comments you receive from customers are a great opportunity to think about how you can improve your pattern or download to make things clearer for future customers — saving you time and improving your customers' overall experience.

When you start selling digital downloads, you might also find yourself answering customer's technical questions.

'You'd be surprised how many people do not know how to download and open a PDF or are unsure how to change their printer settings from portrait to landscape', Claudine says. She includes step-by-step directions in the email buyers receive with their files.

Jenny also recommends becoming familiar with the printing process and colour modes your customers might be using. 'Send your designs to various printers so you can see how they turn out and anticipate what your customers will experience', Jenny says.

Pricing

How do you place a value on a digital item?

That question can be difficult to answer if you're just getting started selling downloads. Jenny started by thinking about how much she would have charged for the art if she had printed it, packaged it and mailed it.

She also considered how much time she puts into each design and what she would consider a reasonable profit to reach her prices of $5.40 USD for single prints and $10.80 USD for sets. Then, she added on expenses like Etsy fees to settle on a final price.

'I feel like my customers have been pleased with the price they're paying', Jenny says. 'Many have come back and said it was so efficient and it cost them less than if they had purchased a print and had to wait for it to arrive in the mail.'

Another concern is that selling digital downloads might take away from sale of your other products on Etsy, but Sarah says it's unwarranted.

'I was nervous to start selling sewing patterns because I didn't want to take away from my lingerie sales, but I found that it's two different markets', she says.

'The people who want to make their own lingerie are not the same people who are going to buy made-to-order lingerie.'

Offering digital downloads can help you add more listings to your shop, reach different audiences and explore new sales channels.

It might also save you some time, so you can focus on creating new products and designs. 'It frees you up to focus on the creative stuff', Jenny says. 'I'm having so much fun with it and I'm growing as an artist and a designer.'

LIST PLACE ON AIRBNB

A new Airbnb or short-term rental venture will yield social capital and, of course, financial capital – both without necessarily requiring any investments on your end.

There are a number of roads you can go down to maximize the benefits of property management that await, and any road leading to Airbnb success begins with publishing your first listing.

Of course, you can always optimize and recruit additional help along the way, but don't run to this solution before doing everything you can by yourself.

With that, I present you with this step-by-step guide to take you through the process of perfecting your first listing from its very inception.

There's no reason to get overwhelmed: the work you need to put into creating your listing is the only work necessary.

Once the listing is completed and published, you can hand over the keys to drive your Airbnb listing towards more bookings, with hands-off account management. Now, onto the slight collaboration needed on your end.

Getting Started

First things first: head to airbnb.com and select the 'list your space' option in the top right corner of the homepage.

You'll be directed to a form prompting you to fill in the most general criteria of your place. Take note that you can only complete this first form prior to creating an account, so it may be more efficient to sign up (or log in) before you begin.

If you have not yet signed up or logged in, you'll be prompted to input your information at this point.

Home Type: These options are pretty straightforward. To avoid any confusion, Airbnb added a brief description of each home type that appears when your mouse hovers over.

Select the option that best describes the property you are managing. Keep in mind that the drop-down menu to the right expands your list of choices pretty significantly, including everything from loft to castles, tents, and so forth.

Room Type: This distinction is one of the most important, as both you and your guests may be particular about maintaining a certain level of privacy.

So, make sure that you're accurately building your listing as to attract the most appropriate guests for your property.

Like with the home type, Airbnb provides short definitions of their room terminology to help guide you through selecting the option that best describes your accommodation.

Before choosing "Entire home/apartment," consider the fact that granting guests exclusive access to your place might include access to other amenities on the property, such as a pool house or a garage.

Similarly, the "Private room" option includes more home sharing than you might typically expect, such as that of any connecting rooms, bathrooms, or kitchens. In addition, you will not be able to edit the number of beds offered in this listing unless you select 'Entire home/apt'; the other options will automatically register your property with 1 bed.

Accommodates: This menu allows you to select the maximum number of people that can comfortably fit in your listing.

For now, calculate how many people you can accommodate if each has his or her own bed, sofa bed, or inflatable mattress, provided that the sleeping arrangement is as comfortable as you would expect if you were the guest yourself.

Finally, select the appropriate number from the drop-down list given.

City: Once you begin typing the name of the city where your place resides, Airbnb will automatically suggest all relevant matches. Choose one, press 'Continue', and move on to the next step.

Now you've arrived at the hub of your listing's more specific details. Airbnb has split this next step into sections, so it will be easiest to cover all information if you take it from the top and fill out the sections in the order that they appear on the list.

Sure to include every appropriate feature as some guests can be swayed by certain extras, or uninterested due to a lack thereof.

If you're totally lost here, refer to this resource for the essentials that every host should include in order to maximize an Airbnb experience.

The Listing

Most of these listing details should already be filled in for you if the first steps are done properly.

You can edit every item unless you're listing only a single room (either private or shared), in which case the number of bedrooms will be pre-registered as and unchangeable as

Location

Simply input the location of your listing and voilà, you've completed the Airbnb listing process.

Once you begin typing your address, Airbnb will suggest the remaining details to autofill for convenience and accuracy.

After your location is filled in, Airbnb will prompt you with a box to add directions and generate a section below with a notice of your local property laws for reference.

As noted on the sidebar, the indicated location will not be viewable to the public, so you don't have to be concerned with any private information circulating around the web.

Instead, on your listing, a circle will appear on a map at the bottom of your listing to give an idea of your area and neighborhood.

When you've finished all this and are happy with your listing, you're ready to be published on Airbnb.

One thing to keep in mind is to always be honest in your description: it won't take long for the truth to come out once your guests arrive.

However, it will be helpful for you to try and spin the not-so-good features of your place in a positive light whenever possible.

Here's the best news: at this point, you have the option to wash your hands of managing your listing.

Guesty can take care of everything for you from here, providing one inclusive and intuitive platform for listing optimization, guest & staff communication, booking management and more.

What would it mean for you? It would mean that the only work you have to do as an Airbnb host is already behind you. Go ahead – sign up for a demo with Guesty and see for yourself!

www.ingramcontent.com/pod-product-compliance
Lightning Source LLC
Chambersburg PA
CBHW021435210526
45463CB00002B/521